# Clay Projects for Children

**Newcastle Libraries and Information Service**

**☎ 0845 002 0336**

8\07 .

| Due for return | Due for return | Due for return |
|---|---|---|
| − 3 JAN 200 | | |
| | | |

Please return this item to any of Newcastle's Libraries by the last
date shown above. If not requested by another customer the loan
can be renewed, you can do this by phone, post or in person.
**Charges may be made for late returns.**

Monika Krumbach

# Clay Projects for Children

## A Practical Handbook
## for School and the Home

A&C Black · London

First published in Great Britain in 2007
A & C Black Publishers
38 Soho Square
London W1D 3HB
**www.acblack.com**

ISBN 978 0 7136 8197 0

Copyright © 2004 Hanusch Verlag
English translation copyright © 2007 A&C Black

A CIP catalogue record for this book is available
from the British Library

The author and publishers have composed and checked the contents of
this book with the utmost care and to the best of their knowledge.
However, under no circumstances can they be held responsible for any
damage or injury which may occur in connection with the book. Working
with clay entails the use of a wide variety of tools and materials, and it is
therefore expressly advised that all projects described in this book are carried out under adult supervision. Please take care to avoid any injury
through sharp objects (tools etc.) or problematic materials (glaze powders
etc.). Children must never be allowed to operate a kiln alone. Ensure you
always comply with local fire regulations.

The author and publishers wish to thank everyone who has contributed to this
book: all the children who allowed us to photograph the highlights of their
collections and who tested all the instructions with us; Doris and Martin
Krottenthaler of Nuremburg who made their wonderful studio available for the
photographs; Barbara Kerzel and the Haus der Begegnung in Erlangern; Rainer
Edelmann and the people from the K4 ceramics workshop, Nuremburg.

Specialist editor: Wolf Mathes
House editor: Dieter Krumbach
Design: Martin Kring

Photographs by Monika and Dieter Krumbach. Drawings by Monika Krumbach

Printed in Poland by Druckerei Dimograf, Bielsk-Biala

# Contents

# A World in Clay

Our multi-coloured, virtual world is defined by short-lived activities and distractions. Manual occupations are becoming ever less important. This is just the point of clay. In an unimaginable number of ways it shows us the power of our own hands. Through modelling from nature we learn to understand the world, and as our fingers mould the clay our imagination takes shape in reality. Few people can resist the fascination of this material.

Earth, water, fire and air – in the ceramic process we encounter all four elements, as the clay connects us in the most tangible way to the environment from which it stems. It has a positive and calming effect, and teaches patience and reflection in a broader context – while waiting for an object to dry, and in the excitement of the firing process with its often unimagined results. Moreover, the timeless quality of the material takes us back to an earlier age when ceramic objects were imbued with exceptional meaning.

This book takes an imaginary journey through the world of clay in a sequence of short, interrelated activities. Follow the route for a systematic introduction to the material, and a variety of projects gradually increasing in difficulty. You will encounter all the vital subjects, from acquiring or gathering one's own clay, making tools and learning the most reliable modelling techniques, to glazing and firing. Technical details are given only when relevant to an individual object and in a manner that can be understood by children. Factual explanations of the important basic techniques and passages of background information alternate with step-by-step instructions for hands-on projects. Interesting tips and tricks ensure that these are both successful and enjoyable. Many of the projects involve amusing,

usable or decorative objects with a special appeal, whether for play or for music-making, with moveable parts or with unusual resonances of the plant or animal world.

Some of the activities are designed to foster collaborative teamwork, others as individual tasks. They are equally suitable for children's ceramic courses, for the school classroom and for relaxing pastimes at home. Most suggestions can easily be adapted to the age and previous experience of the children. While in the nursery school the focus is on playful experimentation and personal expression as the children feel, squeeze and mould the clay, older children put more importance on visible, polished results. This book will provide both groups with a wealth of appropriate ideas and inspiration, which more advanced students can develop into their own experiments. After an initial demonstration, the children can be encouraged to work largely independently, and precision is generally not an issue. Before carrying out any of the individual projects please read the general information at the beginning of the book. Please also note that not all results need necessarily be fired and many of the objects can also be made out of self-hardening modelling dough or the types that you bake in a domestic oven.

We sincerely hope that our boundless enthusiasm for clay will leap at you from every page and that you will find plenty of inspiration for expanding your own creative ideas for working with children. Have fun with trying it all out!

# The Familiarisation Process:
# 1. Finding, Preparing, Experimenting

## What is clay?

It is hard to believe that this soft, pliable mass, which can be played about with and moulded so wonderfully, was originally solid rock! Ancient igneous or metamorphic rock such as granite is weathered by the effects of rain, frost and the pressure and movement of the earth's core. Over the course of millions of years the rock decays into the finest flat chips; mixed with water, these become clay.

The clay either builds up into thick layers at its source (for instance, in the case of pure white kaolin) or else it is washed away by melt waters and rivers, or even blown on the wind, and collects elsewhere in low-lying areas and sunken ground or in river estuaries. It is through this process that the clay tends to gather impurities or additional minerals from the environment. For example, reddish tones indicate the presence of iron.

Large quantities of clay are to be found in every corner of the globe. The different make-up of each individual type determines the colour (white, grey, yellow, ochre, red, brown, black) and also its firing properties. When the mass contains a large quantity of sand and organic matter then we speak of natural clay, or clay loam. Loam too can be modelled with ease, but it is not suitable for firing.

## The four elements

Working with clay connects us intimately with the four elements: earth and water together form the pliable raw material; air dries and shrinks the modelled object, and finally, fire makes it rigid and durable. The creative process involves continual movement, as hands transform a rough lump into the most intricate of figures; as air circulates around the walls and allows the water contained within the clay to evaporate, and as the effect of fire

changes the finest of microstructures, colour and consistency. From decomposed rock to the fired object, clay never stops coming and going!

## What is ceramic?

It is not until the clay has been formed into an object and stabilised through firing that we speak of ceramic. The heat effects chemical changes which leave the walls rigid. We just have to look around us, ceramic is everywhere: crockery, porcelain, flowerpots, toilet pans and bathroom tiles, bricks at a building site and tiles on the roofs of our houses. It is hard to imagine everyday life without all of these. Clay can be modelled by hand or on the wheel, pressed or cast into moulds. Varying results arise according to the material you start out with and the temperature at which it is fired. The walls either remain porous or are rendered watertight through high-firing temperatures or the application of a glaze. In industry too ceramic materials are indispensable – think for instance of gigantic acid-resistant waste pipes, porcelain insulators for electrical wiring, or even false teeth! In earlier times the potter's profession was a common one, as we are reminded today by the widespread occurrence of related family or street names: Potter, Tiler, Clayman, Pantile Street, Potter's Yard, etc.

## Buying clay

The specialist trade and various mail-order suppliers offer a huge range of different clays, mixed and ready to use. Medium-grade 'grogged' (i.e., strengthened with the addition of fired clay particles) varieties are perfectly adequate for use with beginners. Only a few of the objects presented in this book require the finer, 'ungrogged' (unblended) types. Some firms will deliver reasonably-priced 'school clay' in a varying

## Preparing the clay

- Immediately before use, cut manageable lumps off the main roll. Beat this repeatedly on the table surface and knead it gently to ensure a uniform consistency and to get rid of any air bubbles.

- If the clay is too soft, form it into a slab and leave it to dry out a little before use.

- Knead a small amount of fired clay particles into any clay that is too fine or 'greasy' in consistency.

- If the clay is too hard, form it into a thick slab and work the fingers in all over the surface. Pour a little water into the resulting depressions and press the clay back together in several layers.

- Store all clay in tightly closed plastic bags, preferably placing these in a chest with a lid. Label any individual bags.

range of compositions. Smaller amounts can be acquired at a local arts and crafts shop or, in some cases, from a pottery or brickyard.

### Gathering your own clay

Wherever the landscape looks promising, children can be taken out on walks to search for their own clay. They will have heard how the material originates and can work out for themselves where it is most likely to be found: open areas with exposed earth such as fields, building sites, sand or gravel pits; sites of former landslides; river banks and sloping sea coasts offer the most promise. (Please only choose permitted sites where clay may be gathered safely.) Place names can sometimes indicate the position of a former claypit.

My children once even discovered clumps of a sticky turquoise loam in grandma's flowerbed.

## Tip

Any clay that has become hard and unusable should be left to dry out completely, after which it can soaked in a bowl of water until completely saturated, then kneaded as before.

Admittedly, these turned out to be too crumbly to mould easily and only produced tiny pieces. On the other hand, while out walking in the mountains they came upon some beautifully thick, pale grey deposits and on their return immediately moulded little bowls which actually held their shape in firing and turned pale pink! On another occasion they climbed through the narrow opening of a cave only to plunge their hands and knees directly into an invitingly soft mass of clay ...

In most cases gathered clay requires considerable preparation before it becomes usable. Calciferous impurities – known as 'calc-spars' – will cause the walls of an object to burst after firing.

## Preparing gathered clay

- Allow the clumps of clay to dry out completely, then break them into little pieces.

- Leave them to dissolve in a bucket of water.

- Pour the resulting porridge-like slurry through an old wide-meshed kitchen sieve and leave to settle for at least a day.

- Pour off any excess water and spread the slurry in a wide bowl made of plaster or porous clay. Leave it to dry for several days until it becomes pliable.

- Place in plastic bags and leave to rest for a few days, then shape and knead it as usual.

*Knock and squeeze, burrow inside with the fingers, and a lump of clay becomes an inviting cave.*

## Testing clay

Whether it has been bought or gathered from nature, clay arrives in the studio in many different consistencies. As we have seen, not every different type is suitable for every purpose. In the past, experienced potters would actually chew a little lump in order to identify its properties. We have a variety of entertaining ways to test the different types of clay at our disposal:

### Gravity

Hold a ball of clay at head height and let it drop to the ground: the better the ball holds its shape and the less it frays at the edges, the better suited it is for the modelling process. Another way of checking the plasticity is to make a ring out of a rolled sausage of clay.

### The stroking test

Halve a ball of clay with the cutting wire and stroke the flat surfaces with a wet hand: are these completely smooth or do they contain tiny rough particles? At the same time one can tell if the clay still contains any air bubbles.

### The throwing test

Make fist-sized balls of clay and have fun throwing them against vertical surfaces (a tiled wall, a tree trunk, a shed wall): which surface do they cling to best; how long do they stay there? Please only do this experiment where any mess can easily be cleaned up!

### Treading clay

In earlier times several potters would together knead a quantity of raw clay into a smooth mass with their feet. Legs are much stronger than arms, after all. This method is best tried out in the outdoors. Fill a large tub with several kilos of clay and tread with bare feet, placing heels at the centre and working outwards in a fan pattern, as if treading grapes.

### The primordial soup

Take fist-sized lumps of soft or dry clay and place each in a glass of water: it will crack, burst, crumble and in time turn to slip. Which pieces disintegrate the fastest; what colour does the water go; what is left of the lump at the end of the day? Stir the contents of a jar and blow firmly into it with straws from all sides. This process helps us imagine what it must have been like in prehistoric times when the clay was soaked in river beds.

### The weathering process

For an intriguing experiment lasting several months place an unfired clay model (e.g., a piece that has gone wrong) outside where it is exposed to the elements and observe how it gradually decays: the rain washes little particles away, frost produces a

*The primordial soup bubbles away happily. The jars in the background contain clay slops from yesterday, which have already settled noticeably.*

The Familiarisation Process

fine web of cracks, summer heat causes the walls to burst. Document the transformation with photographs taken at regular intervals.

### The shrinking test

Make three slabs of equal size, about 5 x 5 x 1cm (2 x 2 x ½ in.). Store one in plastic wrap and leave the other two to dry in the air, firing one of these two once dry. At each new stage you will observe how the slab becomes smaller and changes in colour occur.

## After firing

As a final test the children can compare fired pieces to determine their different properties. Collect together a variety of ceramic pieces and shards, then blindfold the children and ask them to feel each piece carefully and describe it. A good way to test whether the clay body is still porous is to touch it with the tongue to see if it sticks a little. Watertight (the technical term is sintered) bodies cannot be scratched with a knife.

# The Familiarisation Process 2: Playing and Experimenting

*[the Powenz children] … spent all day bowling around in the gutter, absorbing nourishment from the soil through their pores much as plants do; from the soil, sand, and especially mud, for they had a deep love for water. Water, earth, wind and fire were their favourite playthings.*

Ernst Penzoldt:
*The Powenz Papers:*
*Zoology of a Family*

Children need little encouragement to investigate the raw material of clay. As soon as they have a clump in their hands they begin to poke it with their fingers, to knead, squeeze and mould it. This process becomes even more exciting with a few well-planned tasks. Such individual and collaborative activities serve both to reveal the secrets of clay modelling and to encourage team work within the group. The aim here is not yet to produce lasting results but simply to enjoy the material and to dismantle any inhibitions. The important hand movements and the fundamentals of working with clay are acquired in an intuitive, playful way. Please discuss the tips given in the introduction with the children briefly before they start, and always leave enough time after the exercise to allow the children to describe their feelings and impressions, as well as any difficulties they may have encountered.

## Individual activities

### Totem poles
While listening to the introductory information about the material and techniques, the children each receive a decent fist-sized ball of clay, which they

proceed to model with fingers and tools to their heart's content, the only constraint being that they should not lose sight of the basic form. At the end of the activity the balls are all threaded like giant beads onto a broomstick, then fired and displayed as a vertical column. Older children may need further suggestions, such as to work the ball with their eyes shut, or to make it express their current mood. Can the others guess what they are trying to express?

### Pot-holing
Each child is given a lump of clay weighing around a kilo (roughly 2 lb) and they explore the inside of the clay with their fingers. There arises a system of caves with passageways, halls and multiple openings which can later be explored by the hands and eyes of the other children. Where fingers can no longer reach, the inner walls can be smoothed by means of damp cotton buds and modelling sticks. The outsides are pinched and puckered to look like rough stone. Large caves can be inhabited by any manner of clay or toy figures, and they need not necessarily be fired. The process can be made even more intriguing for the youngest if a few small objects (marbles, nuts and bolts) are buried in the clay beforehand for little fingers to discover.

## Group activities

### Teamwork
The group sits around the worktable and has at its disposal a large lump of clay weighing several kilos. All the children work together on the same lump, the only conditions being that they work in silence, do not remove any clay

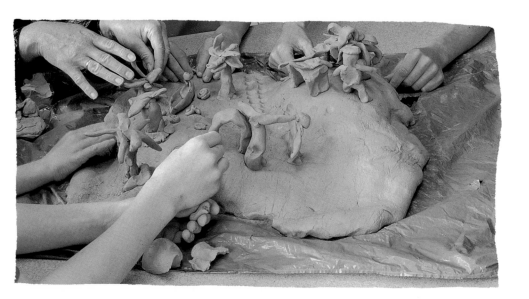

from the original lump, and do not do anything to upset anyone else! The results will be an intriguing series of abstract shapes or imaginary scenes.

## Mountains

In a similar fashion the group works on a rounded clump of clay, with the aim of creating a mountain range. This time the children are allowed to discuss what they are doing. They create winding roads over narrow passes, clefts and valley floors, crosses on the summits and caves, ski slopes and tunnels. If desired the mountains can be inhabited by play figures, and again the work need not necessarily be fired.

## Paradise island

In a shallow plastic tub with a little water lies a large hank of clay weighing at least 10 kg (22 lb). Shipwrecked sailors inhabit the deserted island and establish shelters, vegetation, paths and look-out towers. Each child can mark out their own piece of land with matchsticks, or everyone works together. The result is a wildly romantic imaginary landscape.

## Tip

The island experiment, which brings the children into the closest of contact with clay, is an ideal activity for school or nursery celebrations.

# Some advice on handling clay

## In the workshop

- Where possible the children should wear protective overalls; otherwise, any dried-on clay and splashes of glaze can generally be brushed off or washed out of clothing.
- Work on large, sturdy tables, and have all tools and slip standing ready in jars in the middle.
- Provide each child with his or her own work board of plywood or chipboard (roughly 40 x 40 cm/16 x 16 in.). For particularly sticky masses, a sheet of newspaper can be placed on top of this.
- Water and a container for scraps should be within easy reach. When working with large amounts of clay always insert a fine sieve in the sink drainer to avoid the pipes clogging up over time.
- Ensure that the room is not overheated, so the clay does not dry out too quickly.

## Organisation

- Discuss the project with the children in advance. Always have some ideas prepared, but nothing written in stone!
- With larger groups work with only one sort of clay during each session, or chaos will ensue.
- The clay should be neither too hard nor too soft. You don't want it crumbly or full of tears, but neither should it be sticking to the fingers.
- Mark the finished pieces for identification: each child can devise a personal symbol – like a real professional – with which to inscribe the bottom of his or her pieces.
- Wrap any unfinished pieces carefully in plastic bags during breaks. In this way they will remain fresh and ready to be continued for days or even weeks.

*Lots of hands and lots of clay: anything could happen next!*

The Familiarisation Process

## Modelling

- Always knead and beat the clay a little to begin with to get rid of any remaining air bubbles. If a hollow does appear in the wall of the object later, insert a needle into it to allow the air to escape and then smooth over the hole.
- Keep hands dry while modelling! Never smear pieces in water to smooth them off.
- As far as possible make the objects and walls of vessels of an even thickness.
- Avoid any really thin or intricate details which could break off easily.
- Propose not only small objects but also large, generous-sized pieces where precision is unimportant.
- Pierce large pieces with walls of more than 3 cm (1½in.) thick with a needle or small wooden stick several times in unobtrusive places to ensure that they dry evenly.
- Where hollow pockets have been made intentionally, pierce a tiny air canal into each one.
- When joining two pieces ensure the seams are good and strong: with clay that is relatively wet rough each edge with a fork and then brush on a little water mixed with vinegar before pressing the two pieces together and smoothing the joins.
- When joining two pieces of drier clay, stick the two edges together with a little slip. (To make slip: mix clay and water to a liquid paste and keep handy in a screw-top jar.)
- Do not work on any piece for too long or the clay will become crumbly. It is worth bearing in mind that clay has a 'memory'; in other words, if it has been worked into too many different shapes, it tends to return to an earlier form during the drying and firing process.

## Finishing

- Smooth over surfaces and particularly any edges with fingers or a wooden tool. At the leatherhard stage, this can be done with a metal kidney or a blunt knife blade.
- Alternatively, rub over any bumps or inconsistencies with a damp sponge.
- Compression: if the intention is to hide any traces of the modelling process, the exterior of vessel walls can be beaten smooth all over when leatherhard with a flat wooden bat, a wooden spoon or other implement.

- Please take shrinkage into account when making anything to a particular size. Depending on the type of clay, the body will reduce during drying and firing by around 10–20%.
- When leaving an object to dry place several layers of newspaper between it and the surface on which it stands.
- Before the first firing leave finished pieces to dry slowly and evenly in a cool room – depending on the size, for between one to two weeks. (For firing, see pp. 116–21.)

## Health and safety

- Never leave children to work unsupervised.
- Watch that no one puts clay, tools or any other substances in their mouth.
- Avoid breathing in dust while in the workshop; it is best to do any mixing of glazes, powdered clay or other substances before the children arrive. In cases where children are present, provide them with protective masks.
- Never use materials containing harmful chemicals. Always choose lead-free glazes!
- Store all materials in clearly labelled containers with a tight lid, not in bags or sacks.
- Do not permit eating and drinking during the session.
- Wash hands thoroughly after working, applying cream if necessary.
- Avoid the use of sharp tools or ceramic shards.
- The kiln should only be operated by an experienced adult: make it a hard and fast rule that children never approach the kiln unsupervised.

## Environmental concerns

- Use up any remaining scraps of clay immediately rather than throwing them away; make beads or little animals for instance.
- Wrap larger remnants well in plastic sheets or bags and store in a cool place for later use.
- Any discarded mistakes or dried-out scraps can be reconstituted at a later date. Mixing different sorts of clay is not a problem here.
- Give hands and implements an initial wash with a brush in a large tub of water instead of putting them straight under running water. Recycle the resulting slops of clay.
- Clean glazing implements in buckets in the same

The Familiarisation Process    15

way and reuse the remains for experimental glazes.

- Dispose of any unusable remnants of clay or glazes appropriately (by taking them to the local recycling centre if possible).
- Don't put everything in the kiln indiscriminately; only fire the true successes.
- Make optimal use of the kiln by filling it completely (avoid overloading however). For the first firing the wares can be packed closely and stacked on top of each other.

## Repairing accidents

- Breakages in raw, unfired clay: brush both edges of the break with a little vinegar and stick together with slip. Do not touch again until after firing.
- It is better to give up on any complete disasters straight away. Potters working on the wheel speak of them tenderly as 'the deceased'.
- Breakages after the first firing: make a paste out of a few drops of sodium nitrate mixed with powdered kaolin; dampen the edges of the break lightly with water and stick together using the

paste. Fire again at a higher temperature with or without glaze.

- Breakages after the second firing: stick back together using the above method and fire again. Alternatively use a specialist glue and do not re-fire.

### Tip

Shards from broken pots or plaques can make interesting mosaics: stick pieces to terracotta plant pots using tile glue and smooth over with grout.

*Photo right: Collected works: as an added extra, the children mount a pin-board with sketches and photos of their successful pots and models. Equally appealing is a group scrapbook documenting their projects, or even a proper display mounted in a showcase for public viewing.*

  The Familiarisation Process

# Making your own tools

The most important modelling tools are the hands, and often they are enough. The professionals add in all sorts of specialised implements, but for beginners we need only a few extra aids. Often these can be pinched from the kitchen drawer and adapted to a new use: e.g., a rolling pin for making flat slabs; old forks for roughing edges; knives for smoothing surfaces; kebab sticks, etc. We also make simple tools to fit our exact needs. This always makes for an enjoyable activity prior to modelling, but please take care when using any sharp objects for the initial shaping. For smaller children it is advisable to saw the wooden pieces in advance and leave only the sanding and finishing to them.

## Cutting wires

For cutting off small amounts from a large mass of clay: take a piece of thin wire, nylon thread or even better an old guitar string and attach a cork or a large button to each end.

## Wooden implements

Sticks, scrapers and kidneys for modelling and for detail; make an assortment of little shaping tools from remnants of hardwood, lolly sticks, sturdy twigs with the bark removed, slices from branches or split bamboo canes. Smooth them with a file and sandpaper and shape in various ways; rounded or pointed ends; wide and flat for scraping, etc. Rub with a finishing oil (or olive oil will do) to repel moisture.

## Flat wooden bats

These flat tools are used in a repeated tapping action to compress and strengthen the walls of pots. Take a thick strip of wood, round it off at the edges with a file and sand until smooth.

## Potter's needles

Insert a tapestry needle into a cork. The resulting tool is not as sharp as a real potter's needle and thus is safe enough even for the younger children to use.

## Rotating work surfaces

Bowls, dishes and figures can be worked on more effectively if they can be turned continually. The pros have round wooden discs specially made for this purpose. We make do with a flat wooden base on top of two plastic bags.

## Brushes for applying coloured slips and glazes

Bind little bunches of pine needles or thick tufts of grass or wool to a wooden stick with string or a tight rubber band. Prepare several models in varying sizes for different effects.

*Home made*

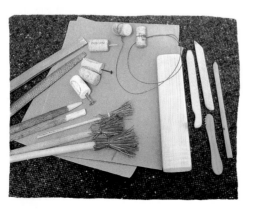

*Found around the house*

*There is nothing more inviting than a well-equipped professional workshop. In summer it can also be fun to work outdoors – preferably in the shade of some trees, in order that the clay does not dry out too quickly.*

## Guidelines for pottery courses

Every child is assigned his or her own designated workplace. Each session should be based around an appealing theme which the children can follow with their own adaptations. It is important in introducing this theme to provide a variety of options and also to leave enough room for the children's own imaginations. Prepare an item on which to 'hang' the project, in the form of a story, a little role-play involving animals, or a selection of images (slides, picture books). An outline is suggested below for a typical course of eight units, each of 90-120 minutes' duration. It is best to organise the glazing of all the resulting pieces as a distinct unit at the very end, in order to avoid confusion and frustration.

1 Introduction, initial experimentation and possibly a group activity from the introductory chapter of the book, in order for the children to familiarise themselves with the material.

2 Modelling figures: With a fairy-tale or animal story as a springboard, the children use the basic skills acquired during the first session to make people or animals.

3 Coiling or pinch-pot techniques: Bowl, tea bowl or dish, decorated with coloured slip, taking inspiration from images of domestic pots from ancient cultures, for instance.

4 Relief techniques: experimentation with stamps, followed by a choice of a self portrait representing a favourite hobby or a footprint from Mars (see p. 62).

5 Building: A group project to construct an African village, where possible out of doors.

6 Musical instruments: various options are offered, such as simple drums, rattles, a zither or a little pipe.

7 Large-scale figurative project following the children's own ideas (e.g. a shoe, a group of figures, a bird house).

8 Glazing and finishing.

The Familiarisation Process 19

# Project: Three-dimensional mountain puzzle

We saw in the introduction how the earth's surface consists of many widely varying layers – interspersed with sheets of rock, sand and humus there are also layers of clay and loam. Illustrations showing such cross-sections of earth and rock can be found in encyclopaedias and geology books. The layers do not run evenly, but sweep up and down and in many places have been contorted into distinctive folds. We can try to imitate this effect with clay. The more different-coloured and structured masses you can use for this exercise, the more interesting will be the resulting mountain. In addition, the project reveals just how different are the properties of each sort of clay: some change colour completely in the course of the drying and firing process; others hardly at all. Heavily grogged 'thin' bodies shrink less than the really fine 'fat' types. For this reason, the occasional separation of layers can occur during firing. Really large mountains need not necessarily be fired.

## Here's how it's done

- Gather together small lumps of all sorts of different clays with similar firing properties, then roll these into balls.

- Increase the variety by mixing two different sorts together through thorough kneading and batting.

- Dye small amounts of white clay by kneading in coloured slip or – if available – some oxide powder.

- Work fired particles of different-coloured clay into some of the balls, or use coloured sand.

- Roughly mix two different clays together to produce marbled patterns.

- Roll all the resulting balls into slabs of varying thicknesses.

- Build the slabs up in layers, incorporating folds and irregular angles. Paint a little slip between each layer so that they hold together well.

- Knock the constructed block together thoroughly with the hands, squeezing gently and throwing it on to the work surface from all sides in order to combine the layers well and to ensure that they do not separate during firing. Work it into an angular mountain shape as you go along.

- Leave it to dry a little and knock it against the surface once more.

- Cut it into eight cubes using the cutting wire, making the horizontal cuts slope downwards slightly into the middle to prevent the top cubes from sliding off later.

- Pierce the inner surfaces of each cube in several places with a needle.

- Reconstruct the mountain and leave it to dry out very slowly. Scrape the outer surfaces once more with a knife when dry, to reveal any grain patterns that may have been smudged during the modelling.

- Fire once. The colours will be noticeably bolder.

- If necessary smooth the surfaces off once more with a piece of sandpaper.

- Use the scraps to make aromatic stones, or gather them into a ball for later use.

  The Familiarisation Process

## Aromatic stones

- Make rough cubes with irregular layers as for the mountain, measuring around 6–10 cm (2–4 in.) on all sides.
- Press the handle of a wooden spoon into the middle from the upper surface, making a canal with a diameter a little wider than the cork which you are planning to use as a stopper.
- Fire aromatic stones only once; do not glaze. Pour a few drops of a fragrant essential oil into the opening and close with the stopper.

*Above and below left: the clay mountain before and after firing. The striking colour contrasts are clearly visible. The pattern of different layers makes for an intriguing puzzle.*

*Below right: These angular aromatic stones are quick to make. The essential oil inside diffuses slowly through the porous walls and fills the room with a delicate fragrance. The opening can be closed with a small cork or a decoratively modelled clay stopper.*

# Basic Form 1: Spheres

We begin our modelling techniques with a shape so basic and natural, it almost happens by accident. The children make simple balls with as many different types of body and colour as possible, including any natural clay or loam gathered on outings into the country. There are two methods: either roll the clay gently between the hands, or on a board. In both cases, take care not to press too hard and thereby create tears and wrinkles. The balls can either just be left to dry as they are or modelled further and then fired. For pieces larger than 5 cm (2 in.) in diameter please remember to prick all over to avoid them exploding in the kiln.

## Marbles

Paint smaller balls with an array of coloured slips (p. 26) and scratch patterns into the surface. Pierced with a hole they become beads.

## Magic balls

Children will enjoy making these balls with a colourful inner life, just as they love to make them out of synthetic modelling materials. Squash together little pieces of different clays, then envelop this central core with a layer of one colour and roll into a smooth, inconspicuous ball. Once it is leatherhard cut it in half with a knife, thus revealing some surprising, chance patterns.

## Animal and human heads

The first step towards modelling from life: attach features such as eyes, ears and snouts with a little slip and immediately the balls come to life. Make a little hollow at the neck with the handle of a wooden spoon. The easiest way to work on the heads is by resting them on the end of a wooden stick. Depending on the size, the results can be made into character-like stick or finger puppets; pencil tops or handles for salad servers; or lids for little tins and pots. For simple stick puppets, drape scraps of material such as bits of old lace, handkerchiefs etc. around the wooden stick and glue the head onto the top. Indicate the hands by drawing up the top corners of the garment into little twists and securing with rubber bands. These little heads also make ideal hand puppets; simply manipulate with a finger rather than the stick.

## Variations on the sphere

Adapt the compact balls into further basic shapes by rolling or pressing, tapping and squeezing. Roll the ball out into an oval, sharpening it into a cone shape at one end, or make it into a nice fat sausage. Older children can experiment with making geometric shapes such as cylinders, cubes, rhomboids and pyramids without taking away or adding any clay.

*One big happy family: Mum, grandpa, Lucy, Joe and Uncle Brian. Fix the modelled clay heads on wooden rods and drape in fabric remnants for a set of easily-manipulated puppets. In no time at all your improvised theatre will be in full flow.*

## Simple animal shapes

You can create a whole zoo from a collection of modified shapes such as cones and ovals, or with balls stuck together to suggest another form. There are many animals which can be represented with such basic forms, and by sticking to essential features the models remain compact yet expressive.

The balls for this activity should be small enough to fit into a child's hand. Stick on any little details, making these from the same consistency of clay as the original ball. Rough both surfaces with a fork, comb or wooden implement before sticking, then dampen and press together firmly, twisting gently back and forth if necessary until the two edges no longer come apart. Smooth over any joins.

# From spheres come half-spheres

After the ball activities you may still have a few soft examples left in various sizes which can take a little more pummelling. The children stand on sturdy stools and drop the balls of clay from outstretched arms onto a wooden board on the floor: immediately you have a series of lovely mountains and domes. Equally, you could simply cut a slightly harder ball in half and work it into a dome by tapping it a little on a flat surface. Here are some appealing tasks:

## Mountains

Take a larger dome and cover it with gullies and paths, peaks or volcanic craters. Stick felt or cork to the underside and use as a paperweight.

*Freshly modelled candle holders: the hole is made slightly wider than the candle, so that it will still fit in after firing.*

## Candle-holders

Make a hollow for the candle with a wooden stick and decorate the sides however you wish. Why not make a whole set while you are about it?

## Picture or place-card holder

Using stiff card, make a radial slit in the upper part of the dome. Decorate the walls imaginatively, fire it, and there you have a simple and adaptable clip for photos or postcards.

## A series of reliefs

Make an attractive set of cane-tops or wall decorations by flattening out a few domes and decorating the fronts in variations on a theme. Before leaving them to dry make a loose hole on the under edge for resting the finished object on the cane or stick. Some favourite themes: animal heads; insects; flowers; sun, moon and stars.

*A simple idea can make a big impression: Slice into half-spheres to make novel holders for photos or postcards.*

## Tip

Many of the projects presented in this book can be made with other synthetic modelling materials or even with homemade salt dough. Only crockery intended for use or any outdoor objects need actually be fired. You will find a wide range of products in larger craft stores and specialist art suppliers, some of which are barely distinguishable from true clay. Some dry simply in the air; others need to be baked in a domestic oven; some never dry out and can be used again and again. Please bear in mind however that these materials are generally less durable than ceramic. The results can be painted according to the manufacturer's instructions with poster paints or with environment-friendly lacquers.

# Painting with coloured slip

Coloured slip is the ideal decorative substance for children's ceramic adventures. In contrast to glaze, it enables even the youngest to decorate their own works. Coloured slips can be used for fine detail and do not run; they can be employed in small quantities and in enclosed spaces; they are safe and economical and since they do not stick during the firing process the pieces can be painted all over, even on the base. Best of all, the children get to see immediate results, with no long wait between modelling and decoration.

Coloured slip is available both in powder form and as ready-mixed paste. In essence it is simply a slurry made from fired clay particles and water which has been coloured with various different materials. It is applied before the first firing onto the raw body – mostly at the leatherhard, but also at the bone-hard stage, or even after the first firing. The numerous bold shades are easily mixed together, and one colour can overlap another. The salmon-coloured shades create skin tones for faces and bodies. Here are a few simple methods ideal for children:

## Application techniques

- Apply the coloured slip with small strokes or in spots; more dabbing than brushing. The pastes have a different consistency to the poster paints that children are used to.

- Ideally let the children try the colours out first on the underside of an object or on some shards.

- Dab the colours on with a small sponge for a thin cloudy layer or a speckled pattern.

- Apply a quantity of slip to a leatherhard surface, then drag a wave pattern through it with fingers or a cardboard comb, or alternatively draw little lines with a matchstick.

- For a splattered effect with thin slip, place the clay body onto a horizontal surface, and allow individual colours to drop from a paint brush held above it.

Basic Forms

- Spray fine spots from a toothbrush or stiff-haired paintbrush.
- 'Wanted' plates: the children model plates out of light-coloured clay (see p. 48), then dip bare hands and feet into coloured slip and press onto the leatherhard surface. Inscribe with a suitable 'wanted' notice.
- Tear or cut thin paper into rough strips and lay these on to the surface of a leatherhard clay body (they will cling easily of their own accord). Dab coloured slip over the strips and then remove them (cf. glazing techniques, pp 105–7).

## Finishing

- Left as they are after the first firing, the surfaces painted with coloured slip remain rough in texture with muted tones. They are good for decorative figures or animals, but unsuitable for crockery intended for use. If fired again at a higher temperature (without any additional glaze), the colours will become more intense. For solid, shiny colours apply a colourless layer of matt or glossy transparent glaze. For a hazy, soft effect wash a thin layer of a transparent coloured glaze over the original decoration.

*A game of chance: where will the splashes of coloured slip end up?*

# Basic form 2: Body bowls

The easiest method of modelling a vessel of any sort is simply to press a ball or thick slab of clay over an already existing form. So why not start with our own bodies? The result will be a series of characterful, unique bowls with interesting organic shapes. 'Mammoth bowls' make a satisfying introductory exercise for children and young people who are convinced they have no 'talent' for ceramics.

## Mammoth Bowls

Gently flatten a lump of firm, grogged clay weighing about 0.5–1 kg (½–1 lb) and press it firmly over a bent knee. Work on bare skin if possible, or protect clothing with a sheet of plastic film or a piece of cloth. Work deep grooves into the outside by clasping tight with the hands and really digging the fingers in. Glaze the inside of the finished object with bright colours.

## Knee bowls

Press a large lump of clay over a rounded knee. Smooth the walls down and stretch them evenly to produce quite a voluminous bowl. For plant pots pierce a drainage hole in the bottom and level it off a little. Allow the bowls to dry upside down over the bottom of a glass jar or similar in order that they do not lose their shape.

## Elbow bowls

In the past potters would occasionally use a sharply bent elbow for the rapid production of tea bowls.

*Who has the nicest knee?*

Basic Forms

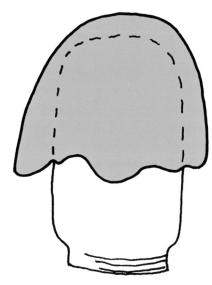

Whoever chooses to can make a set of matching bowls in this fashion from small balls of clay, smoothing each one over with care.

## Avocado cups

Take an oval-shaped slab of clay and, according to body size, press it over a bent knee or elbow to form a slightly cone-shaped bowl. Alternatively, mould it directly over a large avocado. Fire and glaze the finished object.

## Further experiments

Have fun trying out other body parts (a heel or the back of the skull) and natural forms as a negative: a knobbly pumpkin for example, a melon or an interesting piece of driftwood or shape picked up outside. Slip a nylon stocking or other thin material over the shape before moulding for ease of removal.

*Leave body bowls to dry upside down.*

*The plants feel at home in unglazed knee bowls with porous walls. They are decorated with imprints of eucalyptus fruit as well as a lotto counter and a gingko leaf. At the left of the picture you see part of a mammoth bowl, with the pattern made by a clasped hand clearly visible on the outer surface.*

# Basic Form 3: thumb techniques

The bowl that results from the pinch-pot or thumb technique imitates perfectly the shape of a cupped hand. This ancient form is of one piece, with no seams, and lies perfectly in the palm of the hand. We mould the clay in peace and concentration and feel the shape instinctively with the fingers, even closing our eyes as we work.

The pinch pot is a perfectly rounded and aesthetically pleasing object in its own right. At the same time however it is a shape which invites further modelling and forms the basis of many of the projects presented in this book. It is perfect for cups, cereal or snack bowls, candle-holders, hanging saucers for small plants, little hurricane lamps and much more.

*With a little patience a ball of clay can be turned into a nice, even little bowl.*

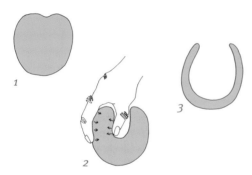

*Maxi, Benjamin and Noah show how it's done.*

## Here's how it's done

- ◎ Mould a smooth fist-sized ball from lightly grogged clay.
- ◎ Holding the ball in the palm of the left hand, make a little hollow in the top with the right thumb.
- ◎ Turn the ball slowly in an anticlockwise direction, meanwhile widening the hole with gentle pressure from the thumb in small rhythmic movements.
- ◎ Thin the walls out through repeated turns by pressing gently in a spiral motion, always working upwards from the base to the top.
- ◎ Apply gentle pressure on the outer walls with the other fingers of the right hand, thus producing an even thickness. The resulting shape will be tall and narrow, a half-globe or wide and flat, depending on the movement and pressure of the fingers.
- ◎ Finish off by stroking the walls upwards inside and out.
- ◎ To achieve completely smooth walls shave them when leatherhard with a scraping tool. Always smooth off any drinking edges finely with the fingers. To make a firm base flatten the bottom off by tapping it gently against the table top.
- ◎ If desired, decorate the thumb-pot with further moulding or applications, and paint with coloured slip or glaze.

*With a handle formed from a protruding lip, the cup sits perfectly in the hand.*

Basic Forms

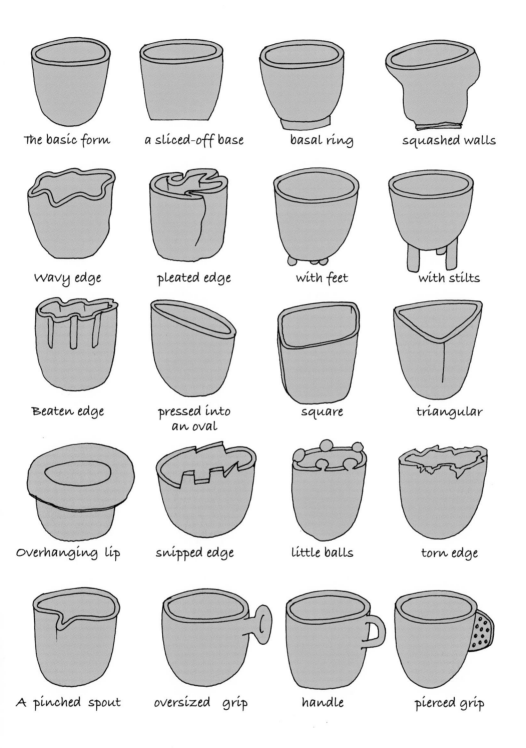

The basic form     a sliced-off base     basal ring     squashed walls

Wavy edge     pleated edge     with feet     with stilts

Beaten edge     pressed into an oval     square     triangular

Overhanging lip     snipped edge     little balls     torn edge

A pinched spout     oversized grip     handle     pierced grip

*The countless variations in form and the therapeutic possibilities of the thumb technique are explored in Paulus Berensohn's classic* Finding One's Way With Clay, *Hanusch Verlag, Koblenz 2003.*

# Project: Animal jars

## Here's how it's done

- Make small thumb pots, adding an extra strip of clay to the top if small fingers cannot reach far enough inside.
- Squeeze the upper edges a little narrower and cut off sharply so that the lids will sit well.
- Mould tails and feet and stick them on.
- Model the heads from simple balls. Take care not to make the features too heavy, or they will lose their balance, and remember to pierce a few holes in the underside.
- Gently tap the base of the pot against a wooden board.
- Paint with coloured slip, fire and glaze. Place any heads which have been glazed all round on supports in the kiln.

## Tip

Filled with tiny toys or goodies to eat, these little jars make splendid, individual presents. The modelling of realistic animal features is explored further on p. 73.

*The spherical heads make perfectly balanced lids for the animal jars. Depending on their mood, they can survey the world around them or look up at the sky.*

 Basic Forms

# Project: Cups with character

## Here's how it's done

- Mould some handy little thumb pots with wide bases and leave them to dry a while until the clay is no longer soft and flabby.
- Use a little slip to stick on heads, tails, wings, fins etc., or alternatively model the whole surface of the cup in the form of a face. Again take care not to make the details too heavy or the cup will lose its balance.
- Decorate with slip, fire and glaze.

If the pots are to be used for food, please ensure that they are glazed with a safe glaze. Smooth off carefully any edges or corners and ensure that no sharp notches or spikes remain.

### Tip

Larger spider or dinosaur bowls make great plant pots with a prehistoric feel, or can be used for storing all sorts of bits and bobs. Please note that fiddly subjects such as these are intended more for decoration and fun than for actual use.

# A journey to Asia: Pottery Japanese style

## The Asiatic art of pottery

Ceramics have been in widespread use in the Far East for thousands of years. Western cultures imported the most exciting innovations from there; most notably the paper-thin, petal-white porcelain, which during the Baroque age caused a huge sensation in Europe. Only in the last few decades have we in the West become familiar with the Eastern tradition of Raku. This is an interesting firing technique whereby the pieces are removed from the kiln with tongs while still red-hot.

## Ceramics in Japan

Handmade ceramics are still in daily use in modern-day Japan, and potters are respected artists. Traditional kilns are often large structures stretching several metres (yards) in length and which big enough to walk around inside. Sometimes little protective figures are placed on top of the kiln before the fire is lit, or a ceremony is held to ensure a successful firing. The Japanese people have a

*Cha Wan*

special reverence for nature. In ceramics too they prefer the chance results to a perfect design. For instance, a potter might deliberately cut into the lip of a finished bowl, or give it a slight dent. In earlier times accidental cracks in a body would sometimes be filled in with gold.

## Tea bowls

Known as *cha wan* in Japanese, these are designed differently for winter and summer use: either narrow at the top, so the tea doesn't cool too quickly, or good and wide. Sometimes a potter can spend several hours making one bowl. Enormous prices are paid for particularly beautiful pieces.

We decided to have a go at making our own Japanese-inspired drinking bowls. To this end we made thumb-pots and clasped them firmly so that our fingers left clear impressions on the walls. Those with the confidence to do so even threw a thin-walled bowl in the air and caught it carefully again in both hands. The impact after the flight

*Wide summer form*

*Narrow winter form*

Basic Forms

again left an impression of the enveloping fingers. Such individual drinking bowls lie perfectly in the hand and have a special feel to them. You may find you are reluctant to give them away!

Always glaze the insides of tea bowls for reasons of hygiene. The outer walls look good when glazed with simple, chance patterns: a few drops or a big splash of colour; or perhaps a flourish of the paintbrush reminiscent of Eastern lettering.

## The tea ceremony

Real Japanese tea ceremonies are held in little tea houses surrounded by a garden, or in traditionally-furnished rooms. The guests sit on low stools or on mats on the floor. Following a strict series of ritual hand movements, the host prepares from finely-powdered green tea a thick spinach-like brew which he hands to the guests one by one. The point is not simply to entertain others, but also to promote a state of inner peace amidst the stress of everyday life. The hosts are always pleased to have their tea service praised by the guests. And incidentally, no one ever drinks from the 'best' side of the bowl; that would be considered impolite! The Japanese might also hold a tea ceremony to honour a balmy moonlit night, and in the depths of winter children will celebrate a festival of lights by building an igloo in the snow and gathering inside to warm themselves up with hot tea.

We would not presume to imitate either the serious nature or the strict formalities of a tea ceremony. We can however take inspiration from the Japanese tradition by choosing an unusual place in which to drink tea in peace and contemplation from our own beautiful tea bowls. How about under a gnarled old tree in the park, or on a little bridge over a stream?

*Typical Japanese: the irregular shapes with abstract patterns of dabs and splashes appeal perfectly to a child's aesthetic sense.*

# Basic Form 4: Coil techniques

Every child should be introduced to the ancient method of building pots from coils or 'sausages' of clay. It is more time-consuming than the thumb process but allows for all sorts of different wall shapes and curvatures. An important element is the cross-hatching of the edges and careful smoothing of the seams. Lightly grogged bodies are the most suitable for this technique. The first step is for the children to practise rolling sausages from small amounts of clay on a wooden board. It is not at all easy to make an even coil, and the first rule is not to press too hard and squash it flat. Only apply pressure with the right hand, using the left gently to keep the end in line. Coils measuring approx. 1-1.5 cm (⅜–⅝ in.) across are ideal for an average-sized pot.

The vessel is constructed by building the coils upwards in a continual spiral. In order to speed up the process some potters give their coils an oval shape, laying them sideways-on as they build the walls up. To stabilise the structure and give the walls a clean, homogenous appearance they are smoothed off when leatherhard with a flat wooden bat or a metal kidney.

*It is very important to rough the joining edges thoroughly with a fork or comb. Take care when rolling coils not to allow the clay to become too dry.*

# Project: Toothbrush holders

## Here's how it's done

- Flatten a fist-sized piece of clay into a slab of around 1cm (⅜ in.) in thickness. Place this on a small wooden board on top of a plastic bag, to make for easy turning.
- Rough the edges of the slab with cross-hatching, using a comb, fork or wooden stick.
- Roll several coils of clay, each measuring around 30 cm (12 in.) in length and 1cm (⅜ in.) in diameter. Rough each coil on one edge in the same way.
- Start laying a coil onto the outer edge of the base, with the roughed side downwards. Press firmly and smooth the seam off inside and out with the fingers or a wooden tool.
- Build up further coils, always roughening the upper edge before laying on the next round. Turn the pot continually on its board and observe from all sides, in order to create an even shape.

- If the inner join between the base and the first coil appears slightly weak, place a further thin sausage on the inside and smooth together.
- The walls can be given a slight curve by laying each successive coil slightly towards the outside of the previous one.
- When the pot has reached about 12 cm (5 in.) in height, smooth off the walls inside and out.
- Stick on ears, facial features and teeth in a large grin, remembering to roughen the surfaces before application.
- To make the hair cut the bottom off an empty toothpaste tube, fill it with clay and squeeze out thin strands through the top end. Alternatively, try squeezing clay through a garlic press.
- Paint facial features with coloured slip, in particular the white teeth.
- Dry the beakers out, fire, and glaze important details with bright colours.

*A lovely shrunken head! Everything fits inside, and tooth brushing becomes much more fun.*

# Basic Form 5: Hollow vessels

Hollow objects are lighter than solid bodies and can be adapted into all sorts of shapes. There are various ways of creating a hollow form; the first two work best with children.

*Method 1*

### Method 1
Roll a fist-sized ball from relatively firm, grogged clay, and work a hole in the middle using the thumb technique (p. 30). Press the top edges back together with the fingers and close with a little flap of clay. The balls resulting from this method are relatively uneven with thick walls.

*Method 2*

### Method 2
Scrunch up newspaper or tissue paper into a tight ball, tying it tight with some cotton thread if necessary – this core ball will burn off later in the kiln. Wrap thin strips of clay carefully around the paper ball, then tap and smooth the surface to make an even covering.

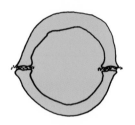

*Method 3*

### Method 3
Make two thumb pots of equal size. Cleanly slice off the rim edges and rough them with cross-hatching before fixing together with a little slip. Clean up the joins.

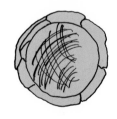

*Method 4*

### Method 4
Cover a solid core (e.g., an orange, a polystyrene ball) with piece of nylon stocking to prevent the clay from sticking. Alternatively, use a blown-up balloon. Cover the central core with an even layer of small slabs or coils of clay, pat and smooth for a finished surface and leave it to dry until almost leatherhard. Cut the ball open at the 'equator', carefully pulling apart the two halves. Remove the core, then close the ball again, taking care to rough the edges before sticking them together with a little slip.

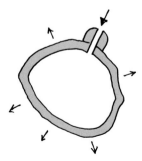

*'blowing up' a sphere'*

## Further modelling

◎ If the ball is too flabby, you can blow it up to make it firmer. To do this, stick on an extra little ball of clay measuring about 2 cm (3/4 in.) across. Pierce a wooden stick through this and into the main body of the ball, then remove the stick and blow air through the resulting canal. Close the canal, cut off the mouthpiece and smooth the surface over once again (see photo).

◎ To make animals or bottles, press and tap the ball into the desired shape.

◎ To make a perfectly smooth ball, hold the leatherhard body in the left hand and tap it all over with a flat wooden bat held in the right.

◎ Once decoration is complete, pierce a tiny hole in the wall of the sphere in order to allow excess air to escape during firing. Dry out completely and fire. Place any spheres with an all-over glaze on supports in the kiln.

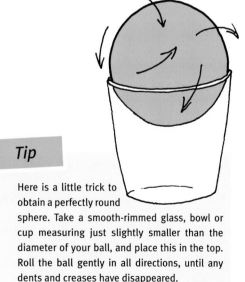

### Tip

Here is a little trick to obtain a perfectly round sphere. Take a smooth-rimmed glass, bowl or cup measuring just slightly smaller than the diameter of your ball, and place this in the top. Roll the ball gently in all directions, until any dents and creases have disappeared.

# Ideas for hollow vessels

*Animal cane-top*

## Cane-tops

Decorate a hollow sphere in the form of an animal, a sun or a face. Attach a ring of clay to the bottom to act as a holder, and after firing place the figure on top of a wooden pole in the garden.

## Little bottles

Attach rings of clay to the top and bottom of a sphere to form the neck and base of the bottle. Work a small round opening into the neck with a needle. Either close with a little cork or make a wedge-shaped stopper from a scrap of clay. Other scraps can be used to make decorations or little pendants to hang around the neck.

## Oil lamps

Model a fist-sized sphere and flatten off the base slightly. Attach a 2-cm (3/4 in.) thick ball of clay to the top to hold the wick and pierce a hole through this with a wooden stick. Cut a slanting hole near the top of the bottle for a cork. Decorate and glaze inside and out. If possible fire at a stoneware temperature in order to ensure the walls are completely

*The little dangling ornaments are attached with so-called Kanthal wire. It can be worked directly into the raw clay and fired while still in place.*

Basic Forms

solid. Thread a piece of wick into the finished lamp, leaving just a little protruding through the opening. Pour lamp oil through the side opening and close with a cork. (Wicks and corks can be found in various sizes in craft shops or specialist suppliers.) Please never leave the lamp to burn unattended.

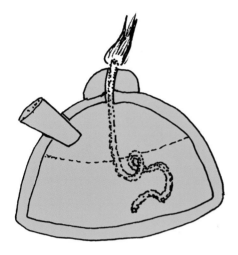

*Oil Lamp: the inside is half-filled with lamp oil (hardware stores). The wick only just appears and is pulled out a little with tweezers each time the flame begins to burn too low.*

*Set the balls spinning to allow them to release their perfume: twist the cord several times and let go.*

## Spinning pot-pourri balls

Make a fist-sized sphere and leave it to dry until leather hard. Pierce two holes in the base and make an opening of about 3 cm (1 in.) in the top. Make a stopper from a 3-cm (1 in.) ball of clay and pierce this with two holes as well. Bore little holes all over the sphere, like a sieve. Fill the fired balls with aromatic herbs or with swabs of cotton wool soaked in essential oils. Thread a ribbon through the four holes in the stopper and the base, as shown in the diagram.

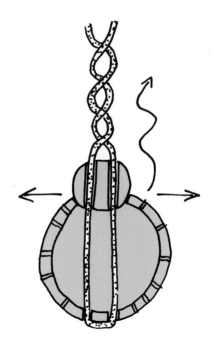

# Project: Bubbling fish

The spectacular inhabitants of the improvised aquarium, blowing cheeky bubbles from pouting mouths, are nothing more than simple hollow bodies. It doesn't matter what size or shape you make them, or whether you seek to create a life-like copy or to follow your imagination. The children can find plenty of examples of brightly-coloured fish by exploring picture books and encyclopaedias.

*Photos provide inspiration for the fish, whether life-like or fantastical in appearance. Coloured slips make for easy and effective decoration.*

## Here's how it's done

◎ Take a lump of relatively firm, grogged clay and mould it roughly into the shape of a fish.

◎ Make a hole for the mouth and hollow out the middle with fingers or a wooden implement, leaving the walls a good 5–7 mm (¼ in.) thick.

◎ Stuff larger fish with scrunched-up newspaper to give them a nicely rounded shape – the paper can remain inside during firing. Smaller fish will keep their shape without the need for stuffing.

Basic Forms

- Close the mouth opening a little with the fingers until you have a hole of around 1cm in diameter.

- Roll a small strip of paper into a tube about 8 mm (⅜ in.) thick and insert it into the mouth of the fish. This will prevent the hole from closing up during further modelling and will allow the body to be blown up again should it start to collapse. You want to ensure that the mouth opening is still approx. 3 mm (⅛ in.) across after firing.

- Refine the shape of the fish, working in curves rather than straight lines, in order to give the finished a object a life-like appearance. Stick on any details such as eyes and fins.

- Create a pattern of scales using modelling tools, paperclips, nail heads or simply the fingers.

- Pierce two holes for a hanging wire in the upper fin.

- Check the walls for any tears and decorate with coloured slip. Dry and fire.

- Glaze your fish with bright colours. It is best to keep the boldest tones for picking out the important details in order that these do not get lost in the whole effect. Place any fish which have been glazed all over on little trivets in the kiln.

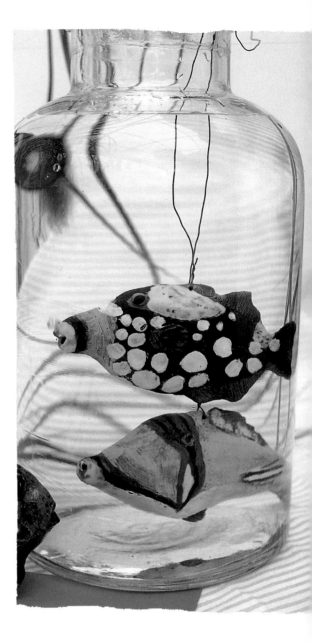

*Goldfish farewell! Grandma's preserving jars are inhabited by brilliant tropical fish. They are fixed to wires and hung from a stick resting on the neck of the jar. As the water slowly enters the belly, a string of bubbles begin to float up from the fish's mouth. If the fish seems to be losing air too quickly, close the mouth slightly with a little candle wax.*

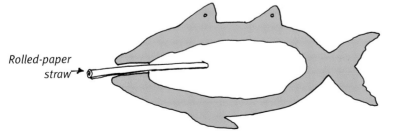

Rolled-paper straw→

# Eating From Your Own Creations

We have learned the most important basic techniques and are now ready to use them in producing our own individual tableware. A glance at archaeological collections and at kitchen practices of the past will reveal how closely pottery has always been associated with food. It was only with the invention of pottery bowls, for instance, that ingredients were able to be mixed up properly and indeed eaten in peace. Food was cooked in various ceramic vessels in the fire.

Examples of ceramic cooking vessels still in use today are the *Römertopf* (an earthenware crock-pot for meat and stews) and the north-African tagine, a bowl-shaped casserole with a domed lid and an integrated stove. In Africa, various such wide-bellied clay pots are also used for the brewing of beer,

*Food tastes twice as good when eaten off your own service, with interchangeable pieces in different designs. The oval plates are decorated with applied motifs in white clay, and colourful glazes.*

*Quick and effective: place-card holders from half-spheres and napkin rings made from simple coils of clay.*

amongst other things. Gigantic urns, taller than a human being, were used in ancient Greece and Rome to store provisions such as wine, oil and grain. By soaking the porous clay walls in water, the contents could be kept cool for long periods by means of evaporation. This method was also common in northern regions before the advent of the refrigerator: for instance in jars for butter and wine. In the course of time, all manner of specialist jars and tableware have been produced from clay.

For reasons of hygiene, all tableware must be glazed. Where possible, use stoneware clay and fire at an appropriately high temperature, in order to ensure that the finished wares are completely watertight. However, a normal glazing temperature is adequate for objects which are intended for occasional use.

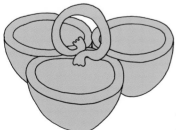

*Snack bowl constructed from three little thumb pots.*

# Project: chocolate fondue from the witch's cauldron

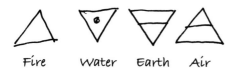

Fire    Water    Earth    Air

## Here's how it's done

- Prepare approximately a kilo (2 lb) of grogged clay.

- Roll out a base to the thickness of a finger and measuring 12 cm (4 ¾ in.) across.

- Build a gently bulging pot from flattened-out coils of clay (see p.36) to a height of 15 cm (6 in.) and with a width of 12 cm (4 ¾ in.) at the top. Smooth the walls and let it dry out a little.

- Model a small thumb bowl with a rounded base, approx 5 cm (2 in.) high and with walls of about 5 mm (¼ in.) thick.

- Widen the top of the bowl and bend gently outwards so that it will hang exactly in the top of the larger pot.

- Make three semi-circular cuts in the lip of the smaller bowl, then hang this inside the larger and mark where the cuts lie.

- Stick three balls of clay to the marked spots on the rim of the large pot and then check that the small bowl can be lifted in and out with ease.

- Leave both pots to dry until almost leatherhard.

- Use a knife to carve an opening for the tea-light in the form of a big jagged flame.

- Cut a series of randomly-spaced flying sparks into the side walls, reaching almost to the rim, in order to allow the candle sufficient air. The easiest way of doing this is to make little triangles with a knife.

- Decorate the large pot with flames in gold-coloured slip and paint or engrave a witch with her broom, a black cat, ravens, etc.

- Allow the whole ensemble to dry and then fire. Glaze the hanging bowl on the inside only, the larger bowl on the outside, leaving the rims free of glaze in order that the two pieces will still fit together well after firing. The distance between the candle and the hanging bowl must still measure a good 6–7cm (2 ½ in.), to prevent the latter from cracking with the heat. (For this same reason do not wash either piece directly before use, to ensure that the porous walls do not contain any moisture).

- Place 1–2 tea-lights in the opening, butter the hanging bowl, fill with 100g (4 oz) of white, milk or dark chocolate broken into pieces and allow to melt slowly over the flame. In the meantime arrange a colourful selection of cut-up fruit in small dishes, then dip them one at a time on little sticks into the fondue.

*Yummy! After a hard morning's magic the little apprentice witches and wizards can lap up some vitamins with their chocolate.*

**Tip**

Make twisted grips for the fondue sticks with left-over scraps of clay, and little dishes for the fruit in mysterious shapes such as eyes, crescent moons, suns or bear paws.

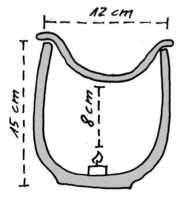

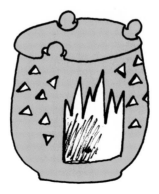

# Crockery with a personal touch

The following examples are easy to make and when used in combination with everyday crockery will liven up many a mealtime. Napkin rings and place-card holders can be made from the scraps.

## Snack bowls

Model three thumb bowls and join them together in the shape of a clover leaf with a ring of clay for the handle.

## Plates

Who says that all plates must be round? Roll out a slab of clay around 7–8 mm (⅜ in.) thick, make cross-hatchings in the surface with a fork and dampen well with a sponge. Make thin sausages from a different-coloured clay and apply these in wild patterns such as snakes or reptiles, etc. Lay a sheet of cling film over the top and roll with the rolling pin. Bend the edges up slightly. Glaze with colourful translucent glazes. Alternatively, cut the rim of the plate into the shape of a star or a flower. Leave the plate to dry out slowly in a shallow bowl or soup plate, so that the curve of the mould transfers itself to your work.

*Piercing holes in a clay wall: a kebab stick and a drinking straw for smaller holes; in the middle a professional tool which carves a hole with a quick twist; on the right an apple corer and a knife for carving triangular windows.*

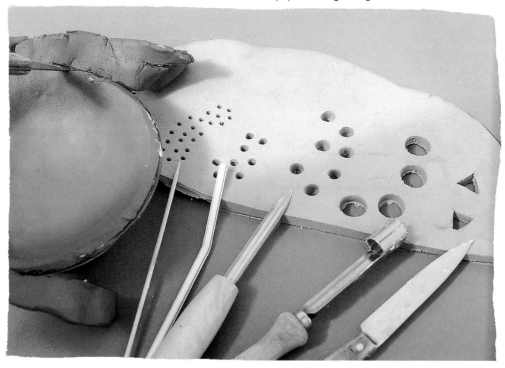

Eating From Your Own Creations

## Breakfast platters

Roll out 1cm- (⅜ in.) thick slabs into oval shapes or cut outlines of animals (fish, whale, fluffed-up birds), then glaze in bright colours.

## Bowls

Shallow bowls immediately look more elegant and will stand more steadily if you apply three little balls for feet.

## 'Living' dishes

Give a muesli bowl a fringe of palms or scatter mice onto a cheese plate or the rim of a dish.

*Make your own delicious curd cheese: First line the clay sieve with a thin layer of muslin. Mix two cups of full-fat or goat's yoghurt with   tsp salt and leave this to drain in the sieve overnight. Squeeze the drained yoghurt in its cloth, then add marjoram or another aromatic herb and roll into balls. Serve with a little olive oil and a garnish of fresh herbs.*

## Goblets

Create tall thumb pots with one or more rings at the bottom as a base. Decorate the walls either with facial features or engrave with abstract patterns, then glaze in bright colours. These are always popular at 'banquets'.

## Dolls' china

Make mini cups and plates for dolls or teddies. In no time you'll have a complete service.

## Serpentine saucers

Roll out a series of clay coils to an equal thickness, then lay them on top of each other in a wild tangle. Knock them flat and roll with the rolling pin.

## Sieve for curd cheese

Make a bowl and matching saucer. For the bowl you can either use coils or a 1-cm (⅜ in.) thick slab pressed into a suitably-sized dish lined with a cloth. Leave to dry until leatherhard, then pierce holes in the bowl at regular intervals and attach three small feet.

# Back to the Bronze Age: An Archaeological Excursion

## A few highlights of ceramic history

*c.* 20,000 BC: Creation of small figures from fired clay in Moravia (part of modern-day Slovakia and the Czech Republic).

*c.* 15,000 BC: Loam sculpture representing two bison modelled in prehistoric France.

*c.* 10,000 BC: The first ceramic vessels are made in Japan.

*c.* 7,000 BC: Clay bricks are used in the construction of houses in Jericho.

*c.* 5,000 BC: Neolithic Europeans develop large hand-made pots (moulded in baskets or made from coils), fired at first in open pits.

*c.* 4,000 BC: Fired bricks are used in house building on Crete (Knossos).

*c.* 4,300-2,700 BC: In northern and central Europe, widespread manufacture of the '*Trichterbecher*', a characteristic funnel-necked goblet decorated with deeply engraved geometric patterns.

*c.* 3,600 BC: Development of the potter's wheel in Mesopotamia.

*c.* 2,500-2200 BC: Typical bell-shaped pots come into use in Europe

*c.* 2,500 BC: First appearance of ceramics in South America.

*c.* 1,000 BC: First use of simple glaze techniques in Egypt.

*c.* 800 BC: The age of the famous Greek vases with their elaborate painted ornament.

1st century AD: Mass production of crockery for everyday use in the Roman provinces. With the development of urban centres comes the establishment of specialized potteries, the smoke from which makes them unpopular.

*c.* AD650: Development of porcelain in China.

5th–8th century AD: Production in Central Europe of the angular Germanic buckle-walled jars (*Knickwandgefässe*), turned on a potter's wheel.

15th century The development of stoneware, increasingly popular on account of its durability.

*c.* 1710: The first European production of porcelain.

1808: The first ever porcelain tooth is manufactured in Paris.

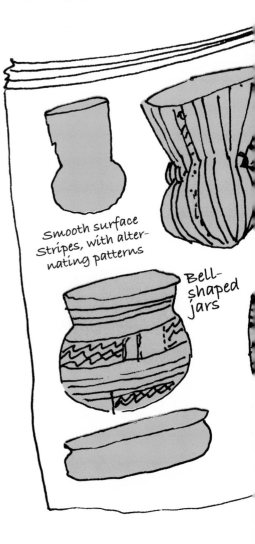

Smooth surface

Stripes, with alternating patterns

Bell-shaped jars

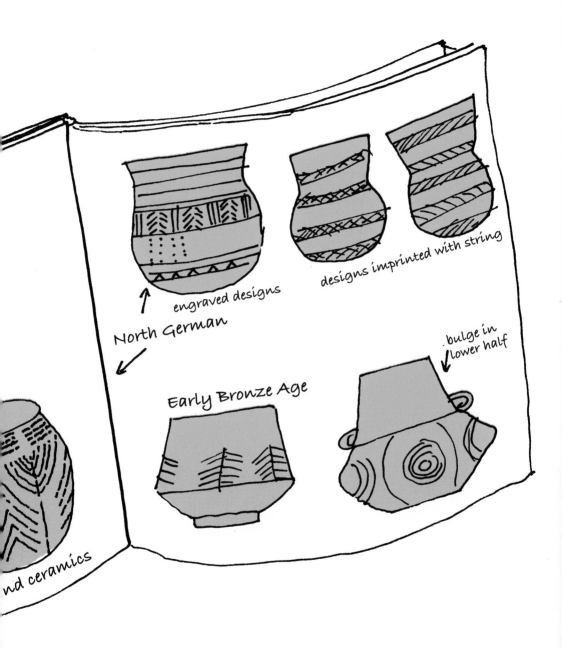

engraved designs

designs imprinted with string

North German

Early Bronze Age

bulge in lower half

nd ceramics

On visits to the local museum or in archaeological books we come across a wealth of interesting pots. We copy the best examples into our sketchbooks, making a note of colouring and size, in order to build our own versions later. We also take time to reflect on their original uses and whether any of the designs are still in production today.

# A visit to the archaeological museum

The history of ceramics, both ancient and modern, provides an endless source of inspiration for potters. Ceramics have been in use in almost every corner of the world for thousands of years and every culture has developed its own distinctive style. Throughout the ages clay has been a vital and versatile material; before the modern era of metal and plastic it defined all aspects of everyday life, providing everything from a family's cooking pots and tableware to the building materials for their houses. Last but not least, it provided our forbears with a crucial means of expressing their inner world in the creation of figurative sculpture and decorative ornament.

In contrast to other materials, fired clay is virtually invulnerable to decay, changing very little even after being buried for thousands of years. Thus we have objects in our museums today which lead us directly back to ancient times, and new specimens are being dug up all the time. Broken pots can be pieced together like a jigsaw and restored to their original form.

A brief excursion into the history of ceramics immediately becomes more hands-on if you set out to make miniature copies of the historical specimens and experiment with authentic decorative techniques, such as engraving and string-imprints. The models can be made quite quickly from simple pinch pots and form an attractive exhibit when arranged on shelves or in display cases. They give an impressive idea of the many versatile and imaginative ceramic techniques of people from earlier cultures. Through our own reinterpretation of historical objects we gain real insight into the lives of our ancestors, whether the original models are bowls from the Germanic Bronze Age, a tablet adorned with Assyrian cuneiform script, or an oil lamp from Ancient Rome.

## Ageing a surface

There is no need to glaze these miniature models. Instead they can be painted in authentic fashion with a thin layer of coloured or plain slip. To give them a suitably ancient-looking patina, smear them with a solution of plaster, soil or clay-loam and wipe off.

Many pots from ancient cultures are either completely black or slightly smoky in appearance. This comes from the type of firing known as 'reduction', whereby they were fired in covered pits in the earth.

# Basic Form 6: Slabs and Relief Techniques

With their many and various uses, clay slabs form the basis of plates, wall and roof tiles, masks, wall decorations, pen pots, or individual plaques for house names. They provide a good-sized surface to be cut up and shaped into various forms, or on which to apply relief ornament.

## Production

Use the hands to flatten out an evenly mixed, well-kneaded ball of clay, using a wooden board as a work surface. Roll the clay out evenly with a rolling pin, taking care not to press too hard and always working diagonally from the outside in, so as to prevent the edges from being rolled too thin. Pick up the slab regularly throughout the rolling process to prevent sticking and, ideally, place a thin cotton cloth or a piece of newspaper between the clay and the board. To create a slab with a consistently even thickness, place two equally-sized wooden slats either side of the flattened piece of clay and roll over the top of the slats. Circles, rings, squares or indeed any fantastical shapes can be first sketched onto cardboard. The resulting template can then be placed onto the clay and traced around with a knife.

## Ideas for slabs

**Cane tops**

Cut animals, face masks or other figures out of a slab of clay approx. 1cm (3/8 in.) thick. Form a ring about the thickness of a finger from a flattened coil of clay, allowing an extra 15% in the diameter so that the cane will still fit into the ring after firing. Leave both parts to dry until leatherhard and then stick them together with slip. After firing glue a suitable stick or cane into the ring.

### Leaf dishes

Cut out a distinctive leaf shape from the slab. To indicate the veins of the leaf make impressions with open-weave material or string, or engrave with a fine tool. Mould into a gentle curve once leather-hard. Glaze in vivid greens.

### Marionette menagerie

From thin slabs cut out separate pieces (limbs, heads, etc.) to make up animals in the style of string puppets. Pierce a hole in each piece and after firing attach the individual elements loosely with wire (see Christmas decorations, p. 113).

### Plant labels

Create pretty plaques with English and Latin plant names to turn the school garden or a window box into a botanical garden. You can also prepare blank plaques which can be written on at a later date with a porcelain pen (modelling shops, ceramic suppliers) and baked simply in a domestic oven. Please remember to bring the plaques in during winter to protect from frost.

*Galium Odoratum - Woodruff*

### Tip

In order to prevent buckling, leave flat objects to dry slowly in a cool room, or cover with a sheet of polythene. It also helps if you can weigh each piece down with a flat wooden board.

### Letter racks

Roll out a slab to a thickness of about 1cm (3/8 in.) and cut out a rectangular shape with a figure carved at one end (see photo). Make two holes in the top end for hanging and mould the straight end around the spine of a book (protecting it first with a sheet of polythene). Allow to dry like this with the figure standing uppermost.

### Portrait plates

Engrave the slab with a face or a self-portrait and cut out into the shape of a head. Leave to dry in a dish with gently sloping sides. Glaze colourfully and either use for mealtimes or hang on the wall.

# Project: mirror and picture frames

## Here's how it's done

- Buy a supply of square or round mirrors in advance from a glaziers or a hardware store, or alternatively recycle little mirrors from discarded cosmetic compacts.

- Cut a template in the same shape as the mirror, but 20% bigger all round, as the clay will shrink in the kiln. For instance, a round mirror measuring 10 cm (4 in.) in diameter will require a template of roughly 12 cm (4 ¾ in.).

- Roll out a slab of clay to a thickness of 1cm (⅜ in.).

- Turn the slab over and mark a window to be at least 1cm (⅜ in.) smaller all round than the mirror after firing. In other words, for the 10 cm (4 in.) mirror, your window will need to measure approx 9.5 cm (3 in) before firing, giving a final diameter of approx. 8 cm (3 ⅛ in.).

- Cut out the marked window with a sharp knife, carving the outer edge of the frame into your desired shape at the same time – fantastical designs such as a blazing sun or a knight's helmet are always effective.

- Pierce two hanging holes in the top.

- Lay the cardboard template over the window and press hard into the clay until the template and slab are at the same height. Remove template.

- Allow the frame to dry a little. Turn it over and decorate the front with engraved or relief motifs, or with applied ornament.

- Fire and glaze.

- Fix the mirror to the reverse of the frame with all-purpose glue and hang with strong cord or wire.

- Using a washable felt pen, the mirror can be given a different facial expression whenever the weather changes!

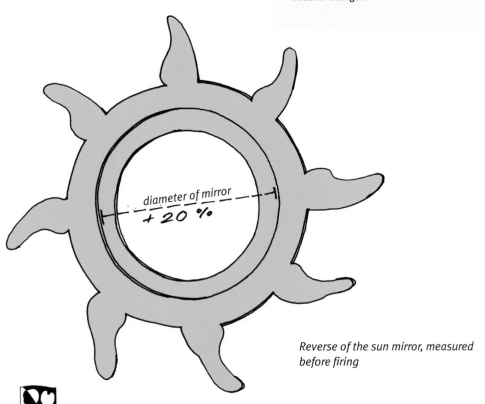

*diameter of mirror + 20 %*

*Reverse of the sun mirror, measured before firing*

Basic Forms

*The sun mirror is on the left. Beneath that is an abstract design hung with little ornaments cut from copper foil. Whoever looks in the knight mirror on the right will see themselves reflected in full armour! In the middle is Dagmar's self-portrait as 'court damsel'.*

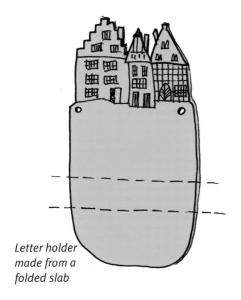

Letter holder
made from a
folded slab

## Tip

Follow the same method to make picture frames. The pictures are stuck on to cardboard and fixed into the window from behind with masking tape.

# Surface design: Stamps and Printing

A clay stamp allows for the repeated, exact reproduction of a single motif; a process which children find hugely fascinating as they discover the great variety of ways in which the raw, still pliable clay can be shaped and textured. Decorative plaques printed with a combination of two- and three-dimensional designs will provide endless creative possibilities, and the process is a satisfyingly direct one with instant and clearly visible results. Gather individual works together to create an entire wall frieze.

Even the first experimental pieces are worth keeping: the little pattern blocks are always satisfying to the touch, and gathered together provide a pleasing sensory memory. Use ungrogged clay to make the stamps, and please always bear in mind when working with stamp patterns that the impression will be reversed on the finished object.

## Experimenting with fingers, tools and scrap materials

Each child is given a slab of clay approx 1–2 cm (⅜ –¾ in.) thick on which to experiment with creating their own repeat patterns. Suggest some of the following methods:

- Pinch with the fingers, smoothing and stroking the clay. Make grooves in the upper surface of the clay, and push up bumps and hillocks from the underside.
- Repeat the same actions with a wooden modelling stick for more definite impressions.
- Print lines, squares and trian-

gles with wooden blocks, working in varying rhythms. For example, print each individual shape directly next to one another or diagonally; close together or with spaces of flat clay in between.
- Press pieces of rough, open-weave material or snippets of lace onto the surface of the clay.
- Scratch patterns into soft or leatherhard clay with a nail or a needle.
- Polish leatherhard surfaces with the back of a spoon.

## Ideas for 'reclaimed' stamps:

- The edges of corrugated card.
- Screw heads; nuts and bolts; cog wheels.
- Pieces of thread or wire, used straight or tied in knots and hammered flat.
- Coins; buttons with a raised pattern.
- Strips of old bicycle tyres; rubber soles, etc.

## Making your own stamps

### From clay

Make a small block of clay, cutting the face side off straight. Leave it to dry slightly then carve or press a design into the face, and fire. The convex patterns will later appear in relief on the imprinted surface.

### From plaster

Stir powdered plaster into water according to the manufacturer's instructions. Pour

*Plaster stamps*

*Relief plaques decorated with coloured slip and under-glaze colours. In the middle a double animal relief (see p. 62).*

the mixture into little cardboard boxes and leave to set. Tear off the cardboard and engrave the smooth surface with your desired motif. The resulting imprint will be more clearly defined than with a clay stamp.

## Rolling seals
Make fat rolls of clay about the size of a film container. When leather hard, carve a design into the curved surface and fire. Roll the seal over a slab of clay for a continuous pattern.

## Lino cuts
Cut a pattern into a small piece of lino and place this onto a soft slab of clay (or a plate, wall plaque, etc.). Roll evenly with the rolling pin to transfer the pattern. If you paint the lino beforehand with a little coloured slip, you will end up with a two-tone image.

## String stamps
Wrap or stick lengths of thick string around a little block of wood and experiment with textured patterns.

## Decorating simple objects

### Tea bowls
Stick a small slab of clay to the outside of the bowl and imprint a design with your own stamp.

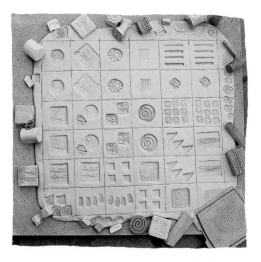

### Fridge Magnets
Stamp an image into a ball of clay, glaze brightly and stick a magnet to the reverse. (Magnets can be bought in a DIY store or metal merchants.)

### Touch memory
Roll out a slab of fine clay to a thickness of 8 cm (3 in.). Using a ruler, mark out a grid of squares 5–6 cm (2–2 ⅜ in.) in size, but do not cut at this stage. Print the squares with your prepared stamps, using each motif twice. Allow the slab to dry a little before cutting up the grid of squares. Smooth the edges of each square with a damp sponge when leatherhard and then fire. Do not glaze, as you want to retain the clear definition of the pattern. Choose the most striking pairs for a sensory memory game in which the blindfolded children have to match up the squares by touch.

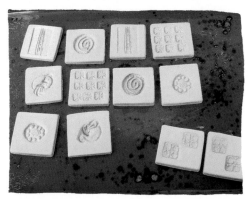

*Photos, middle and bottom:*
*leave the freshly-imprinted grid to dry out a little before cutting into individual squares and the results will be much smoother and more even. See how the fine, ungrogged clay takes up every little detail.*

# Printing from Nature

Let the children begin by leaving their own impressions in soft slabs – a hand slapped down hard or a bare foot pressed into the clay. Depending on the pressure applied, they will see a wide variety between each other's stamps. You could even allow anyone who dares to sink his or her teeth into a lump of fine white clay fresh from the packet (no chewing or swallowing, of course!).

Next ask the children to search the house for suitable stamps to experiment with; they'll find crinkly nut shells, the dimpled peel of citrus fruit, shells from a visit to the seaside and much more. Every child can model his or her own dish with a distinctive nature print stamped in the middle.

Later, perhaps on a woodland walk, the group can go on a proper hunt for natural treasures to print with. Each child should take a plastic bag containing several fist-sized lumps of clay for making impressions on the spot. First they might notice the impressive bark patterns of the trees themselves: deeply furrowed on an oak or a fir tree; smooth and delicately striped on a birch; faintly dimpled on the younger saplings at the edge of the wood. They'll move on to discover the distinctive ring markings of felled trunks, deeply-veined leaves; acorn cups and pine cones; seed pods, twigs, wiry grass stems for printing long loops, and pitted pebbles on the path.

# Project: Display shelves

The most fascinating patterns found by my group of children at the end of one extremely dry summer came – sadly – from drought-ridden trees, where the bark had already begun to peel off in great chunks. The pale wood revealed just the faint traces of bark beetles. On the inside of the strips of bark however the intricate network of their tunnels was clearly visible. The children brought some pieces of bark home with them, brushed any loose fibres off with a stiff brush and left them to dry a little, weighted down with stones.

### Here's how it's done:

- Roll out two slabs of clay to a thickness of approx. 1.5 cm (⅝ in.) one the size of a dinner plate, the other of a saucer.
- Lay the slabs on to the bark with its pattern of tunnels, pressing gently with the hands to ensure that the pattern transfers onto the clay, but without the two surfaces sticking to each other.
- In each of the plates, make three equally-spaced holes, a little wider than the sticks you intend to use for hanging (an apple corer is ideal for this).

*The finished display shelves are decked out with natural finds from the woods. The simple dishes with fossil and bark impressions have handles made from wood and garden wire.*

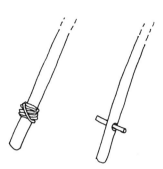

*A knot of string*     *Bore a hole for a little wedge*

Drape the plates into soup dishes to give them a slight curve, and fire when dry.

- Either apply a transparent glaze or simply rub in a little coloured slip or oxide powder before the second firing to highlight the pattern.
- Cut three pliable twigs to equal lengths and wrap a few rounds of string around each one about 3 cm (1 ¼ in.) from the bottom; these will form the rests for the larger plate. The string will stay in

place better if you make a knick in the twig with a knife first.

- Working in pairs, thread the twigs through the holes in the larger plate until it rests on the string, with the long ends of the twigs projecting upwards.
- Thread on the smaller plate and mark where it needs to rest in order to be able to gather the twigs together in tepee fashion at the top. Attach a further three rounds of string to the marked spots.
- When you are happy that both plates are sitting level, bind the twigs together at the top.

## Fossil platters

Roll out irregular lumps of white clay into rough-edged slabs. Make impressions with twigs, ferns, ridged shells, rough stones, fish bones, etc. Paint the biscuit-fired platters with thin green and brown-coloured slip, then wipe it off and fire again. The resulting dull patina gives the impression of a real prehistoric artefact.

*Impressions of plants, shells and bark-beetle trails*

# High and low relief: 'my favourite hobby' in clay

Images in raised relief are made either with coils of clay or thin cut-out motifs, applied to the slab with slip and outlined with a modelling stick for extra effect. You can make the applications from different-coloured clay if you wish. A bas-relief on the other hand is achieved by engraving a pattern into the slab, carving out either the motif itself or the background. The indented surfaces must remain at least 5 mm (¼ in.) thick. Once the ornamentation is finished, little windows can be cut in the slab to lighten the effect of the relief. Don't forget to make hanging holes.

When it comes to applying colour, it is best not to cover the reliefs with a uniform glaze. Instead, wipe with a thin oxide or coloured slip in order to highlight the pattern, or otherwise brush with a transparent glaze, thus leaving the detail clearly visible.

*Fresh from outer space: This impression comes straight from the red, sand-strewn surface of Mars. The white clay slab reveals whacky footprints of 'extra-terrestrials', which have been printed with a variety of tools, screws etc. Sand was pressed into the surrounding surface before firing. Glaze was applied only to the footprints themselves.*

Surface Designs

## Suggested themes

- A desert scene in ochre-coloured clay with applied snakes, scorpions and other heat-loving animals.
- An ocean scene: comb a wave pattern into a slab of white clay and wash with a transparent blue glaze. Decorate with large sea animals such as whales, seals and sharks made from the same white clay.
- Life beneath our feet: Make a series of labyrinthine tunnels and people them with moles, mice and worms, in high or low relief.
- Figures and scenes from popular fairy tales.
- Visual representations of popular sayings or famous quotations from around the world.

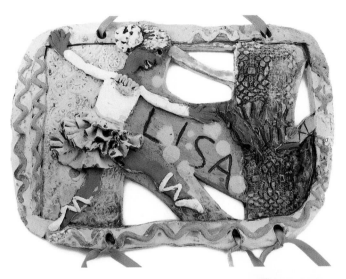

*The different relief techniques have been combined here to produce some vibrant self-portraits. In their enthusiasm the children decided to add some 'genuine articles': Matti spends his whole time riding his bike and has built a real spanner into his work; Lisa has depicted herself as a future prima ballerina, with an impression of lace from her own cardigan in the background. Jurek loves to go fishing with his dad and has included a little guide to some common fish.*

# Making Ceramic Jewellery

Clay beads and jewellery are quick, easy and economical to produce and can be made in any style, from really fine pieces for parties to wild and whacky ethnic creations. Added elements in other materials make for truly spectacular designs. Furthermore, jewellery-making gives the children a chance to try out relief and colouring techniques in mini-format before moving on to larger objects.

## Beads

- Roll clay into little balls and twist each one slowly onto a wooden stick, trimming off any ragged ends. Decorate the beads as desired with coloured slip, engravings or little stamps. Glaze only the upper half of each bead, or otherwise fire them on a special bead support. Large beads are best made with hollow centres so they are not too heavy to wear: wrap a thin layer of clay around a tightly-rolled ball of kitchen paper.
- Some of the very first beads produced by ancient civilisations took the form of an eyeball and were worn as protective amulets: paint beads with a pale glaze and place a darker spot at the centre.

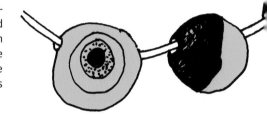

*Pendants with exotic lettering and symbols*

Surface Designs

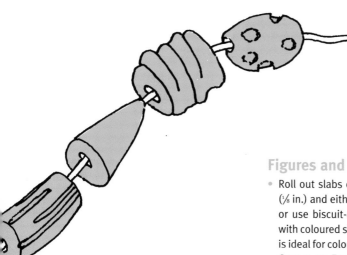

## Figures and amulets

- Roll out slabs of clay to a thickness of 2–3 mm (⅛ in.) and either cut simple shapes with a knife or use biscuit-cutters. Paint or imprint designs with coloured slip or oxide powders. This method is ideal for colourful jewellery inspired by Ancient Greece or Egypt, or Native South and North American cultures.
- Friendship-pendants with initials inscribed in hieroglyphs or in exotic Japanese, Cyrillic or Greek script are always popular with adolescents. They can look for ideas in an encyclopaedia or on the Internet.
- With a supply of brooch pins from a craft shop the children can make flat clay figures into imaginative brooches.

- Lay two strips of contrasting-coloured clay on top of each other and roll out lengthways. Cut off little strips and roll these into 'snails', threading them sideways so as to reveal the stripy pattern.
- Having first threaded round beads onto a stick, mould them into ovals, cones or barrel shapes.

*Beads made from wood and red and yellow felt are intermingled with the heavy ceramic pieces.*

## Making up necklaces

- Use leather thongs or strong cord for threading the beads. Tie a knot between each bead, or alternate with felt shapes or little wooden beads; the aim is to avoid clay knocking on clay. When threading pendants ensure the cord is not too long, to avoid them constantly banging against tables, etc. Leather thongs can be made economically from scraps. Cut a circular piece and trim the edge, cutting in a spiral, to form a continuous strip of about 2–3 mm (⅛ in.) in width.

- To make felt beads, cut strips of felt in contrasting colours, approx. 1cm (⅜ in.) wide and 8 cm (3 ¼ in.) long. Lay the strips on top of one another and roll into a sausage, securing the ends with a little glue. Thread sideways-on to reveal the contrasting snail pattern. Use the imagination in

## Tips

- Use fine, ungrogged clay.
- Pierce the threading hole in each bead slightly above the centre point; this will prevent the bead from spinning round the whole time and hiding the pattern.
- Make sure the holes are large enough and smooth off any rough edges to avoid fraying the thread.
- Remember not to make any piece of jewellery too heavy.

combining clay with other materials: silver wire; glass beads; pieces of bark or small chunks of wood; feathers; shells; coloured string or strips of leather; felt and woollen beads. Decorate brightly-glazed surfaces with further patterns in gold or silver lacquer.

*Small ceramic designs become colourful necklaces, bracelets and ankle bands. Beads and pendants can always be strung in a new way if you become tired of the original arrangement.*

*ABOVE:* Firing rests for beads, home-made from slabs of clay. The glazed beads are suspended on Kanthal wire.

*BELOW:* Wild and wonderful American-Indian jewellery decorated with coloured slip and stamp patterns.

# Modern Art

We tend to associate the idea of modern art less with figurative or decorative objects than with abstract shapes, suggesting either starkly geometric or intriguingly organic forms. As we experiment with and play about with clay we get to know its qualities and possibilities in an immediate and relaxed way. If we allow ourselves simply to be led by the shapes that emerge naturally, we can almost do nothing 'wrong'. Whether due to harmonious proportions or exciting contrasts, the end result is always striking, with the natural interdependence of structural form and surface design creating a pleasing visual unity. The following short tasks can be useful in structuring an activity such as this.

## The clasped hand

Grasp a ball of clay tightly with one hand, making deep impressions with the fingers; use both hands for larger balls. Just this simple gripping action can produce a wide range of different sculptures, each of which can be modelled into further abstract designs and smoothed as desired.

## The block

Each person chooses the accidental shape of a good-sized lump of clay as their starting point. The idea is to stick to the basic form of the original mass, thereby allowing oneself to be led by the ideas suggested by the material itself rather than imposing a design from the outside. The contours can be rounded, modified and perhaps sculpted a little with hands or tools so as to give the form some artistic expression. In addition, you could suggest some adjectives – appropriate to the age and interests of the children – which the clay should be made to express: for example, should the impression be one of peace, grace or fear; excitement, tiredness or anger?

## Mountains and towers

Using wooden slats or battens, or the flat of the hand, knock a large block of partially prepared clay into an angular geometric shape: a tower for example; a pyramid or a rough cube. Press a well into the upper surface and you have a robust and elemental vase for twigs and greenery.

## Organic forms

Here we are following in the footsteps of famous artists such as Henry Moore, Barbara Hepworth or Jean Arp. The children work at giving a lump of clay an organic shape by a process of rounding and smoothing, making hollows and openings, and creating either delicate or monumental contours and swellings. Inspiration can be found in natural forms such as seed pods and fruits, or microscopic pictures of cells. The aim is to create a pleasing object with a clear and simple form, such as could have been produced by Nature herself; an object which asks to be touched and held in the hand.

## Additional materials

The possibilities increase when you alter the structure of the material itself. For instance, you can knead various items such as millet seeds, rice, twists of paper, etc. into the clay before modelling. These will burn away in the kiln and leave interesting textures on the surface of the work.

## Playing with surfaces

Cut into the edges of a slab of clay in several places, then lift up the strips and twist or bend them, sticking them to each other or to the surface in places, until you have an airy, skeletal sculpture.

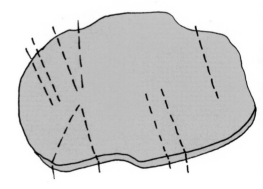

## Mixed Media

In recent years ceramic artists have combined their work increasingly with metal, fabrics and natural materials, often creating interesting collages.

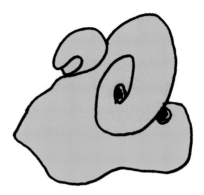

- Twist scraps of cloth, coloured threads, strands of wool, felt or wire, around a piece of clay, perhaps partially disguising a modelled object.
- Give a ceramic work added elegance by mounting it on a block as if on a pedestal (wood, brick, a cobble stone or an interesting found object).
- Integrate natural materials by a process of application, impression or by creating hanging elements.

*Sculpture park. Copper wire or thick garden wire is used to attach several different individual pieces to a larger work. The added elements wave about and bounce up and down.*

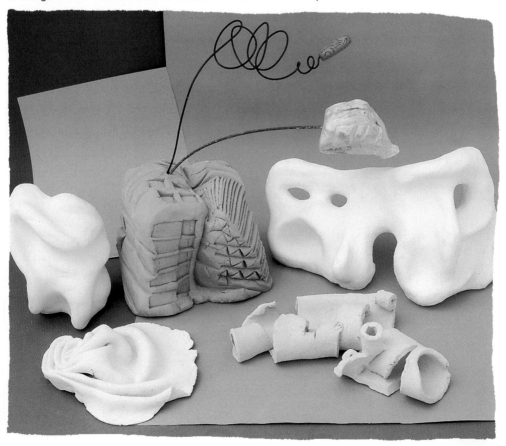

# Modelling Figures:
# Animals, People, Mythical Creatures

Modelling people and, above all, animals, is a popular activity for children of all ages. Many children have their own pet at home and they will be familiar with the more exotic animals from the television. When it comes to imaginative figures, fairy-tale heroes from popular books will always seize the imagination. Having already drawn and painted their favourite characters many a time, clay offers the children a chance to give them three-dimensional form. Start simply by reading a story to put the children in the mood.

With little effort, even mythical or prehistoric creatures can easily become real – whether it be dinosaurs or the Abominable Snowman, unicorns, dragons and mermaids. Finally, the children might like to conjure up their own make-believe characters, working together to come up with suitably imaginative names.

When taking on one of the more demanding forms, the children will need to employ all the tricks of the trade learned so far. The results will be all the more successful if the group takes time beforehand

to concentrate all their senses on the essential traits of the animal in question. What is important here is not so much a beautiful object as an authentic and life-like one.

## Preliminary exercises

One day I asked the children to suggest what they thought were the biggest or smallest, most dangerous, slimiest or cuddliest animals. We began to imi-

*Rhinos on the catwalk: strong personalities all round.*

  Modelling Figures

tate the beasts, each acting out the gestures and characteristic movements of our own favourite. With a little face-painting and some dressing-up the poses became more genuine. We twittered and miaowed, shrieked and roared, slithered and crawled, trotted, stamped and leapt about, and as we did so the individual characteristics of each animal became more and more clear: the massive elegance of the elephant; the fidgetiness of the dormouse, the sedate calm of the giant tortoise. We rejected the usual frogs, owls, penguins, dolphins, robins, squirrels, crocodiles and snakes, and tried instead to represent faithfully the more bizarre species such as deep-sea fish, toucans, anteaters and armadillos.

## The cheeky rhinoceros

After these initial games we decided to agree on one specific animal which each child could then model in their own style. But which was it to be? We had recently seen a film about Africa, full of zebras, guinea fowl and ostriches – but not a single rhinoceros! So the rhino it was to be – especially since we already had a postcard on the wall of the familiar engraving by Albrecht Dürer, the famous son of our home town of Nuremburg. His rhino was the very image of an armoured fighting machine; where, we wondered, did he come across a living model almost 500 years ago?

We learned from an animal encyclopaedia that there are several different types of rhinoceros, and so, armed with drawing materials, we set off for the zoo. There we indeed found a real rhino, but sadly without the most important feature; a horn! The

zoo keeper explained that it had to be regularly trimmed to stop the animal from harming himself.

Finally we ended up in the toy shop and bought a small but very detailed plastic model to help us. We discussed the shape in detail and each made a sketch, in which we attempted to reduce the animal to its basic form. The rump was straightforward, as was the head with the two large horns. Only the face was really tricky, with tiny eyes in comparison to its size and these lying much further forward than one would expect.

# Free Range Beasts: some basic animal shapes

## Cones

Make a tall cone from grogged clay, forming a ball on top for the head. Carve a deep hollow into the cone from the bottom and stuff with newspaper. Either remove this after the object has dried, or simply leave it there to burn away in the kiln. Apply or engrave further details. This method is particularly suitable for animals with a compact upright stance (penguins, birds), or for sitting animals such as dogs and cats. Equally, it is a good way to make people. In the case of really small cones, the hollowing out process is not necessary (see dwarves on pg 89).

## From lumps come rumps

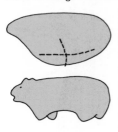

Make an elongated oval from grogged clay, cutting a cross in the underside as illustrated. Form the legs from the rump by pulling the clay gently downwards where you have made the cut. Add further details and leave to dry on a scrunched-up piece of newspaper to prevent the figure from collapsing.

Bore several holes in the underside of the rump and upwards into the legs with a wooden stick, adding any further details after this process.

Alternatively, finish all modelling with the body intact and leave it to dry until leather hard. At this stage, hollow out the underside of the rump with a teaspoon, so nothing can be seen from the side.

Or, model the animal over a ball of newspaper, making the walls approximately 1–2 cm (½ –¾ in.) thick. With this method you need only make a few little holes to allow the air to escape during firing. Leave the model to dry on scrunched-up newspaper.

## Larger shapes

It is easy to model an animal from one large lump of grogged clay. However, it is important that they do not remain too dense, or you risk them bursting in the kiln. Here are three suggestions:

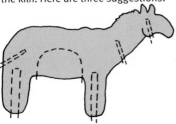

### Tip

With a few holes bored in the top you can turn an animal model into an amusing pen and note-holder for your desk.

# Surfaces

Next to an authentic body shape, it is the numerous clever ways of imitating fur, skin, etc., which give ceramic animals their particular appeal.

**Smooth and shiny:** polish the surface when leatherhard with the back of a spoon. Alternatively, finish with a shiny glaze.

**Rough and matt:** dab the clay all over with a rough-textured material, or sponge on coloured slip, leaving the figure unglazed.

**Knobbly skin:** either poke craters into the surface with a wooden stick or a screw-head, or stick on little balls of clay.

**Scales:** either pinch the clay with your fingers or press a knife blade in at a sideways angle. Alternatively, print a pattern by pressing a piece of plastic netting (e.g., from a net of fruit bought at the supermarket) into the surface.

**Armour plating:** carve a criss-cross pattern of grooves with the edge of a wooden spatula, smoothing over any rough edges afterwards.

**Wrinkles:** draw irregular crossing lines in the surface with a modelling tool, or print a network of little grooves with scrunched-up stiff paper.

**Fur** – various methods: engrave a hair-like pattern with a comb, a stiff brush or a fork; dab slip on roughly with a sponge; extrude thin sausages of hair by working soft clay through a garlic press or an old kitchen sieve.

**Spikes:** either model these individually and stick them on, or snip a series of v-shaped jabs in the surface with a pair of scissors held at an angle. Alternatively, push little spikes of clay upwards from the surface with a thin wooden stick.

*A wide variety of quite realistic skin and fur effects can be achieved with a collection of everyday household objects.*

# Fun and Games with Animals

## How the Hippo took to the water

The hippos thought themselves so ugly, that they asked the god of men and animals if they could spend the day hiding in the water. 'OK' said God, 'then you can just come out to eat at night. But make sure you don't eat any of my fish!' The Hippos were happy with this. And now each time they surface they immediately open their mouths wide, to prove that they really haven't taken any fish. *(Story from Malawi)*

## Spitting llamas

Make a llama with a hollow middle as in the sketch. First make the core from scrunched up newspaper, working into it a thick strand of cotton thread (or a 'string' made of tightly twisted toilet paper) so that it sticks out at both ends. Then model the body around the core, with both ends of the thread appearing from the mouth and tail end. Add on legs and other details. The core and thread will burn away in the kiln, leaving a canal through the whole figure. Fill the inside with water after firing: when you blow through the tail end, the llama will spit, just like in real life!

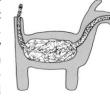

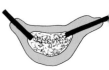

A duck is even easier to make: form a nicely rounded body around the newspaper core then poke a round wooden stick in through the beak and at the tail, and remove.

## Greedy gobblers

From solid lumps of clay, model wide-mouthed animals such as hippos, frogs or whales. Hollow out the inside as far as possible through the mouth and insert their 'catch' for all to see. Make marsupials such as kangaroos in the same way, with their young in a pouch. If you leave the inside empty, the animal can double as a goal: roll up little balls of paper and have fun aiming them at the mouth.

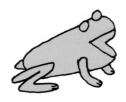

 Modelling Figures

## Swinging monkey

Make a monkey with long curly arms and lay it on its back to dry and for firing. Hang it up in a house-plant jungle.

## Shelf ornaments

Using firm, grogged clay, model animals with long dangling legs and a flat base so they will sit on a shelf or the edge of a table. Hollow out the body from the base and decorate with colourful glazes.

## A double relief

Cut freshly modelled animal figures across or lengthways through the middle and stick both halves to a slab of clay (see also the photo on p. 59).

## Rocking animals

Roll out a round slab of clay measuring about 8–10 cm (3 ⅛ –4 in.) across.

Fold it over in the middle and model a head and tail at each end of the crease. Decorate the sides with engravings and coloured slip. Set it rolling gently on the rounded edges until the movement is smooth and regular. This very simple method works well for birds, ducklings and rocking horses.

## The Loch Ness Monster

Model a little dragon or sea monster and make a depression in the bottom with a wooden rod. Fire, glaze and stick the model to the rod. Find a suitable plastic pot or beaker and cut a cross in the bottom, inserting the rod from above so that it sits quite firmly. Fix a small length of string around the middle of the stick to prevent the beaker from slipping all the way down. Push the beaker upwards and fill it with little balls of blue tissue paper or any other light material (tea leaves, sawdust, confetti, etc) until the monster is completely hidden. Push the stick up and the monster will appear mysteriously from the depths.

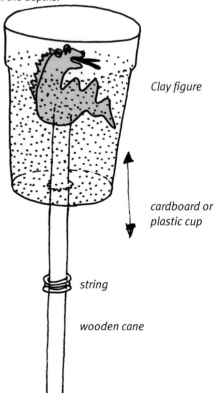

*Clay figure*

*cardboard or plastic cup*

*string*

*wooden cane*

# Human Figures

*The God of the Bible formed 'the people from out of the earth, from the soil of the fields, and blew the breath of life in through their noses'. (Genesis 2, v.7).*

Further attempts along these lines went a little out of control: the Golem, created according to legend by Rabbi Loew of Prague in around 1600, was a figure from clay-loam brought to life, which did not quite match up to the expectations of its master.

We decided to stick with more modest ambitions and concentrate instead on modelling life-like portraits or fantastical characters in miniature. To begin with we studied each other very carefully, observing both physical appearances and individual mannerisms. Typical poses to copy were sitting, standing, squatting or lying positions. We felt each other's heads closely with our hands: where exactly were the bones and the soft parts; the hollows and the bulges?

Young children tend to model the features they consider most important out of proportion to the others. As for the older ones, they are more concerned with the expression of real emotions and facial features. Here are a few suggestions:

### Snowmen
Build simple figures according to the snowman principle, from three balls of clay in differing sizes. Add features and decorate at will. Even three-year-olds can manage this activity.

### Chunky people
Cut into a flattened lump of clay as indicated in the sketch, so that arms and legs separate naturally from the body. Refine any details. These compact figures are sturdy and appear almost as if they have been cast.

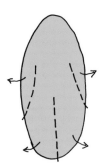

### Rubber men and women
Using different sizes of clay sausages for limbs and trunk you can produce a series of flexible, very life-like figures. Details and features are not necessary here. Dry the more delicate forms flat on their backs so as not to lose their shape. Excellent for dancers, athletes, acrobats and any display of dynamic movement.

### My very own statue
Children from secondary-school age upwards like to make portraits of themselves or each other, sometimes disguised as a famous person. Make the head by wrapping a core of newspaper with a 2-cm (¾ in.) thick layer of clay. Leave the shape open at the bottom and attach a ring for the neck. Model or apply features. After firing, place the work on an improvised pedestal (made from wood, a breeze block or polystyrene) and give it a suitably imposing title.

These portrait busts are perfect for a game of disguises: simply make them a set of flamboyant baroque wigs with long curly locks out of fresh coils of clay, and their looks can be changed at will.

## Life studies

Model life-like fragments of body parts either in their original size or to a smaller scale; an ear, an eye, a hand, for example. Afterwards the group will find it intriguing to compare the enormous differences in the individual interpretations.

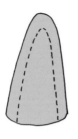

## Dioramas

Each member of the group contributes a figure for a display or group exhibition. The approximate scale of the figures is agreed beforehand, but the rest is up to each individual. The important thing is to choose an appropriate theme that will spark the imagination.

**Some examples:**
- Sun worshipers at the swimming pool or on the beach can be displayed in a tub with real sand.
- Eccentric passengers on the underground sit on little building blocks or polystyrene cubes.
- Disco-goers are kitted out with all sorts of glitzy accessories (aluminium foil, colourful scraps of material, etc.).
- Sleepwalkers stumble about with armfuls of cuddly toys.
- A series of portraits of people with unusual professions.
- An underwater scene with divers, mermaids and mermen: if possible arrange the people in a real fish tank or garden pond.

*Tickets please! Scenes from a tube carriage. White clay, painted with acrylics (designed and modelled by Rainer Edelmann).*

• Little gnomes inhabit a cave made of real roots and branches.

*The little sleepwalker is made from a hollowed-out cone. Arms, feet and details are stuck on.*

## Project: wild woodsmen

... and women. We are not talking about well-behaved, tame, easy-going, sluggish, sleepy people here, but really scary figures and trolls who live in the forest and work as its protectors. Before letting our creativity run wild we try out the best grimaces and mad gestures on each other, in order to be able to model them better.

The figures, measuring approx. 30cm (12 in.) in height, are hollowed out from underneath and stuffed with newspaper in order to help them keep their shape while drying. If they are only given a biscuit firing and are left unglazed, the porous clay – like ordinary flower pots – will develop a green patina after some time in the open; we helped our figures along a little by painting them with diluted low-fat yoghurt. They can be further equipped with twigs and other woodland features. Bring them into the house in winter to avoid them cracking in the frost.

*Armed to the teeth, the wild creatures are on guard in the front garden. With a little luck an authentic patina will develop in damp places.*

# Further Figurative Themes

Using the techniques learned during previous sessions and a bit of 'freestyle' modelling, your students can produce any number of sculptural objects, from life or still-life. They can either come straight from the imagination or are copied from a model. Exotic themes are particularly attractive, but equally so are the ordinary everyday objects, brought into a new light through three-dimensional representation. Children will be most inspired by subjects offering a variety of structures and interpretations. Providing you use coarsely grogged modelling clay, even large and hollow objects can be successful.

Popular interpretations include botanical themes: a forest of baobab trees with a tangle of branches made from coils; cacti and houseplants glazed in bright greens and 'planted' in real pots with sand; stylised seed pods and tree fruits or whole colonies of mushrooms with striking silhouettes. More demanding projects can include ideas such as a series of way-out shoes, or a well-upholstered three-piece suite!

To make boots and shoes, first model the rough shape from a large clump of clay. Then remove the surplus clay from the inside of the shape with the fingers or a blade or wooden tool, before finishing the surfaces and refining the details. Each shoe takes on its own individual personality.

A design-your-own hat project offers a similarly broad playing field, and can result in some stunning contrasts, with glazed and unglazed, smooth and eccentrically decorated surfaces.

*The fantastic shoe store: The surfaces offer plenty of scope for experimenting with colourful glazes.*

# Nature and the Environment

Clay and the natural world belong together. This versatile material fits well into any natural environment, and animals and plants feel at home with it. With little effort we have made individual bowls for our two dogs Bello and Minka, playhouses for the guinea pig, and flat, round-edged water dishes for birds, to hang safely away from cats from the branch of a tree. For hygiene reasons please be sure to glaze all food and water bowls. However, the other objects described in the chapter should all be left unglazed, in order to make them more sympathetic to insects and birds. They are not purely decorative, but can be put to real use. The simple observation of birds and insects can lead children to take a greater interest in the natural world.

## Home-made shelters for wildlife

## 1.Insect hotel

### Here's how it's done

◎ Take a lump of ungrogged clay weighing about 0.4 kg (1 lb) and, working on a wooden board, use your hands and wooden bats to mould it into a rough house shape.

#### Option 1

◎ Using a pencil or a wooden stick make lots of horizontal tunnels through the clay, varying the size from 10 mm (⅜ in.) to 3 cm (1¼ in.) in diameter. Work carefully, turning the wooden tool back and forth so as to achieve a smooth inner surface. As the picture shows, the first inhabitants will soon take up residence.

#### Option 2

◎ Hollow out the house from one side with a spoon, cutting the walls straight with a knife. Make a hole through the gable with a dowel. Smooth all the walls once more inside and out and decorate the outside at will. Allow the clay to dry and then fire, but do not glaze. Thread a hanging wire through the hole at the top. Now fill the inside with short bamboo sticks, reeds or hollow twigs, all in varying sizes. Pack the sticks in well so that they support each other, or alternatively attach them at the back with a little glue or wax.

## 2. A horny nest for earwigs

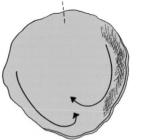

### *Here's how it's done*

- Take a good fist-sized ball of grogged clay and roll it with the rolling pin into a round slab approx. 5 mm (¼ in.) thick.

- For the decoration, either print patterns with leaves, twigs etc., or stick on appliqué designs.

- Make a cone out of newspaper and wrap the slab of clay around it, sticking the overlaps with a little slip and neatening the edges.

- Roll the very tip of the cone into a little snail, leaving a hole in the middle for hanging.

- Make several little holes in the lower edge for the wires to be inserted later.

- Allow the cone to dry around its core of newspaper.

Nature and the Environment

- After firing, stuff the inside densely with wood, wool, straw or moss. Insert a couple of pieces of wire through the prepared holes to prevent the stuffing from falling out.

- Hang the horn upside down in a tree. The cosy dwelling will attract beneficial earwigs. They will spend the day in their house, coming out at night on raids to gobble up lice, greenfly etc.

## 3. Blue-tit café

### Here's how it's done

- IUsing the thumb or coil technique, make a bowl with a rounded base, measuring about 15 cm (6 in.) in diameter at the top.
- Cut a 2–3 cm (¾ –1 ¼ in.) hole in the middle of the dome.
- Decorate the outer surface of the bowl, squeezing it gently into an oval for a beetle or a bird shape.
- Once fired, suspend the bowl upside down over a sturdy branch with several twigs protruding from it to provide support from underneath. Ensure the long end of the branch fits the hole tightly, and secure with a little string.
- Place the construction in a bucket with the open surface of the bowl facing upwards, ready for its contents.
- Melt some lard or bacon fat over a gentle heat on the stove and stir in sunflower seeds, oat flakes and other grains. Fill the bowl to the rim with your prepared concoction and leave to set. (If the stick does not fit the hole of your bowl tightly, fill the gap with a little Blu-tack.)
- Hang the branch back up in a tree, away from the reach of any cats.

*Wild bees and solitary insects seek out pipe-like homes in which to lay eggs and for their young to develop. Our little garden houses were soon full of occupants. The only problem is the blue-tits, who keep coming to see what delicious guests are waiting for them inside!*

# Green-roofed bird table

Set up this romantic bird table in a sheltered place and birds will love to visit it. Please always clean it out before refilling; a simple sweep with a brush will do.

## Here's how it's done

- Prepare about 2.5 kg (5.5 lb) of grogged clay (you will have some left over after cutting out the windows).
- Collect together some moss and cuttings of house leeks or sedums to plant on the roof, along with some sandy soil. You will also need a long wooden pole measuring approx. 2.5 cm (1 in.) across (a broom stick is ideal).

- Roll out a round slab of clay to a diameter of about 20 cm (8 in.) and a thickness of 1.5 cm (⅝ in.).
- Cut a hole in the middle about 4 cm (1½in.) across. The pole must still fit through it after firing.
- Using flattened coils of clay, build up a tall dome shape on top of the round base, smoothing the walls inside and out as you work. Close the opening at the very top with a little lozenge of clay.
- Allow the dome to dry out until almost leather-hard and then tap the walls smooth from the outside with a flat wooden bat.
- Insert the pole through the hole in the base and with the very end press a slight dent in the roof of the dome; this is how the house will later be suspended.
- Model a bird or other ornament to stick on top of the bulge, and make crosshatchings along the top edge of the dome with a fork.
- Make a coil of clay approx. 50 cm (20 in.) long into a flat band of about 3 cm (1¼ in.) in width. Lay this band around the prepared edge of the dome and fix with slip.
- In the crease where the band meets the dome make some downward-draining holes for excess water.
- Using the knife, make some large irregular windows in the side walls. The remaining branch-like pillars need to be at least 3–4 cm (1¼–1½in.) thick to support the roof. Leave the lower edges of the windows rough to create an easy perch for the birds.
- Decorate with appliquéd leaves and incised patterns of veins, tendrils and branches.
- Support the structure while drying with a core of scrunched-up newspaper.
- Fire the construction and then if possible put it through a second firing, but leave it unglazed.
- Ram the wooden pole into the ground in a sheltered place and hang the house over the top. Fill the roof with a little soil and then the plants.

# Fantastic Gardens

Clay harmonises wonderfully with pebbles and plants. With a big moulded dish as your starting point you can create mysterious landscapes for indoors and out, combining natural and fantastical elements however the mood takes you. Chose either of the two following methods to model your dish, and adapt the decorative elements whenever you feel like a change of scene. (Remember to protect in winter from damp and frost.)

**Method 1**
Roll out a base plate of about 1.5 cm (⅝ in.) in thickness. Build up a rim and partitions from thick coils and add any combination of hills, bridges, secret passages, caves and a pond or little lake.

**Method 2**
Knock a football-sized lump of clay into an irregular slab measuring approx 5 cm (2 in.) in thickness. Use a spoon to carve out hollows for fields, gardens and ponds. Allow the work to dry out very slowly as it is so thick.

## A gnome garden

Fill the dish with moss, pebbles, twigs and low-growing plants. If you like, fill one or two of the depressions with damp cotton wool and sow with cress seeds. Half-hidden in the undergrowth arrange little figures  made from natural found objects such as chestnuts or seed pods. Alternatively, make little gnomes out of finger-sized cones of clay.

## A magical garden

Arrange a collection of treasures in the dish, including, for example: coloured sand, semi-precious stones, found objects; marbles, glitter and tinsel; test tubes filled with coloured water (food colouring).

## A water garden

If your dish is glazed, you can plant little specimens of papyrus, rushes, etc. Make a lake and cover it in duckweed, then sail carved bark boats or floating candles on it and arrange real and modelled seashells and snails. For an open-air water garden, dig a hollow in the earth and line it with a 3-cm (1¼in.) thick layer of clay. Divide this layer into different partitions and fill with water and plants as above.

## A desert garden

Fill the dish with sand and stone formations. Add real (or realistic models of) cacti, termite hills in terracotta and even the odd skeleton modelled from white clay!

## Japanese garden

For a meditative, Eastern feel, decorate your garden with pretty natural finds, mini clay sculptures, little lamps, raked sand and (if you happen to have one) a bonsai tree.

## An archaeological site

Create the scene of an archaeological dig by filling your dish with soil and gravel then scattering it with shards of pottery and miniature clay models of urns and jugs (see also p.52).

*A finger-sized cone, two arms, two feet, a simple face, and your little gnome is ready. These playful figures will turn your garden into a magical realm. They are ready in a matter of minutes*

# Musical Ceramics:
# Making Musical Instruments

Wander around any ethnological museum and you will discover an astonishing variety of traditional musical instruments made from clay. A sound is created simply by the vibration of air, and this quality is common to all instruments: it is their individual shape which determines the hugely differing tonal nuances.

Perhaps the best known of pottery instruments are the flutes – from the rounded ocarina typical of the barrel-pipes to the long delicate flutes in the style of wooden recorders. They have been in use for millennia and have a captivating, far-reaching sound. Modelling a pipe or flute with fresh clay enables you to make repeated adjustments until you get the right sound. On the other hand, making ceramic flutes is often a slightly risky activity, as they can occasionally distort during firing and become unusable. In order to avoid disappointment it is a good idea to make several examples of the same model. In addition, since the project relies on precise dimensions, it is worth making an exception to the usual practice here and guiding the work closely yourself rather than leaving the children to experiment alone. Despite all these restrictions, the spectacular results nevertheless make flute-modelling well worth the effort.

Simpler to make are flower-pot-like drums with open bases and a skin made from stretching wet leather over the top. To achieve the optimum sound, they are best played with their bases resting at an angle to the ground. Why not build up an extensive clay orchestra with all sorts of different instruments? Simple wind harps, bells and decorative mobiles hung in the trees or on supports in summer will ring against each other to create a complete tonal garden and can be augmented with metal pipes and bottles, old flower pots, etc. – but please spare a thought for your neighbours!

## A musical mobile

### Here's how it's done

- First prepare the clay: where possible use stoneware clay and fire it at the appropriate temperature to ensure that the individual pieces don't break too easily as they knock together.

- Make a series of flat motifs. For example, roll two different-coloured clays into one strand then cut off slices and press them flat with the hands. Or roll out slabs of clay and cut out imaginative shapes such as birds, leaves or animals. Another motif that is quick and easy to make is the simple stick figure. These are created from thin coils squashed onto a wooden board and lifted off when leather hard.

- Make hanging holes in the top and bottom of each piece.

- Dry, fire, and glaze or decorate with poster paints.

- Make a hanging support and tie each individual piece to it with string, so that they hang just close enough to knock and ring against each other with gentle movement. The higher the firing temperature, the clearer the sound.

- If you like add beads, shells, yoghurt-pot lids and other metallic items to the mobile.

- Hang in a draughty place either outdoors or inside near a door or window.

## Here's how it's done

- For each pipe begin by pressing a fist-sized piece of very soft clay into an elongated shape.
- Take a wooden rod measuring 30–40 cm (12–16 in.) in length and 1.5–2.5 cm (⅝–1 in.) in width and push it through the length of the lump.
- Press and smooth the mass of clay around the rod until the walls are of an even thickness.

- Roll the sausage carefully and without applying any pressure over a wooden board, until the clay covers the rod evenly and firmly.
- Hold the end of the rod and begin to twist the clay sheath gently until it frees itself from the wood.
- Leave the clay to rest a little, still on the stick.
- In the meantime use the scraps of left-over clay to make a hanging support, or decorative beads to string along with the pipes.
- Roll the rod and its clay covering once again over a board to smooth the walls. This will be easier now that the clay is no longer sticking so tightly to the wood.
- Cut a straight edge at either end of the pipe and carefully remove the wooden rod.
- Pierce two little holes for hanging at one end of the pipe.
- Dry and fire, then decorate with coloured slip. If you choose to glaze the pipes, fire them on metal supports to prevent them from sticking to the surface of the kiln.
- Tie the pipes, together with any additional strings of beads, either to the clay support you have prepared or to a branch or wooden pole drilled with holes, positioning them so that they knock together with gentle movement.

*Hang three or four pipes together for a pretty wind-harp with pleasing tones.*

Musical Ceramics

# Here's how it's done

- Take a walnut-sized lump of clay and model a regular, gently widening, bell-shaped pinch pot.

- Allow to dry until almost leatherhard, then smooth walls and edges thoroughly.

- Use any scraps to make beads, little birds and other decorative items, all with a hole for hanging.

- Slice the rim of the bell cleanly with a knife and smooth over once again. The rim determines the clarity of tone and should therefore be especially thin and carefully finished.

- Make a small hanging hole in the top of the bell with a needle.

- To dry the bell, place it upside down in a cup or similar to give it a smooth round form.

- If necessary, polish the walls again after the first firing.

- Glaze inside and out, leaving the rim clear.

- Thread the bell onto a string along with your other ornaments.

- Tie a large bead in the centre of the bell, positioned so that it knocks exactly against the rim.

- Alternatively, tie a series of bells along a wooden rod to create a true 'Glockenspiel'.

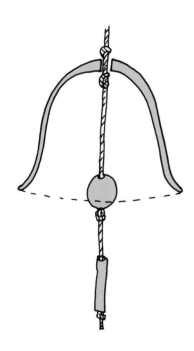

## Maracas

### Here's how it's done

◎ Using a grogged clay that is not too soft, model a round or oval-shaped hollow ball (see techniques on p.38). You will get a particularly nice effect by using a small, firmly blown-up balloon as the core instead of the usual paper. Wrap the core in little slabs of clay, smooth all the joins and tap gently all over to firm up the structure. A needle inserted into the ball will burst the balloon, and it can stay inside during firing.

◎ Insert a couple of pea-sized clay balls (raw or fired) into the body of the – rattle, either through the opening or before fixing the two sides together depending on the method used to create the structure.

◎ Close the opening with a small lozenge of clay, or stick the two halves together with slip, as appropriate.

◎ Clean up the ball and tap it smooth once again.

◎ Make a handle from a long fat coil or loop.

If you roll the coil at a slant on the very edge of the table it will develop an interesting pattern of spiral ridges and will be easier to hold while playing. Any really thick handles should be pierced through lengthways with a thin stick, to avoid them bursting in the kiln.

◎ Allow the ball and the handle to dry out a little and then stick together with slip.

◎ Smooth the surface of the rattle once more and cut decorations from a thin slab of clay. Apply these to the smooth walls with slip and tap firmly to compress the surface.

◎ Make a tiny hole in the rattle with a needle.

◎ Lay it to dry on a few sheets of cling film or tissue paper.

◎ After the first firing, apply glaze to the original surface only, leaving the applications clear. Fire again on supports to prevent the glaze from sticking.

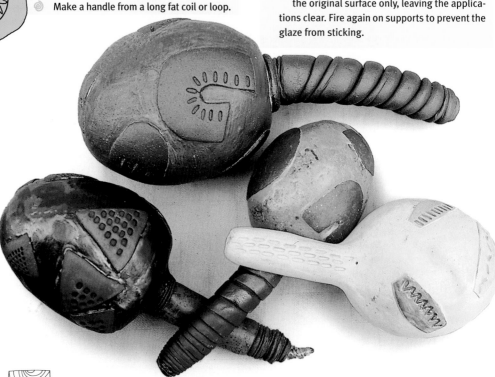

## Tip

An amusing way to make the best of any kiln accidents is to make simple 'shard' rattles. Place the broken fragments in a plastic bag and beat into smaller shards with the rolling pin or a hammer. Sort these according to size into several jars and tins. The different rattles will vary in sound according to the size and composition of the shards.

## Zither fish

## Here's how it's done

- Take a rough clump of clay and form it into a long, simple fish form measuring about 20-30 cm (8–12 in.) in length. Give it a wide base and straight walls about 3–4cm (1¼–1 ⅝ in.) high, and model the tail to act as a handle.
- Mark notches at equal spaces along each side wall.
- Hold the handle of a wooden spoon at an angle to the base and make regular jabs to create a scale pattern.
- Fire and glaze.
- Stretch thick rubber bands (or trouser elastic, etc.) tightly across the body of the fish, fitting them into the notches on each side.
- To play your zither, simply pluck these strings with the fingers: the tighter the rubber bands, the higher the sound. Tune the strings by tightening them if necessary. Placing the fish on a wooden surface will produce a louder sound.

## Here's how it's done

- Using ungrogged clay, form a pear-shaped lump, approx 7–8 cm (2¾–3⅛ in.) long, that sits comfortably in the hand.

- Cut the shape in two vertically down the middle and leave it to rest a while.

- Using a wire loop or a teaspoon, hollow out the inside of each half as in the sketch, smoothing the sides well. The walls should remain about 5mm thick.

- Stick both halves together in their original form with slip. Smooth the joins well.

- Poke a needle through the width of the neck (the mouth piece) to make a hanging hole.

- Allow the structure to rest a little more.

- Make a wooden wedge (cardboard will work if necessary) with a width of 8 mm (⅜ in.) and a point sharpened to a thickness of 2 mm (⅛ in.). Push this down through the neck of the barrel until the point reaches into the hollow interior, resting near the front wall.

- At the bottom of the neck make an opening for the sound hole, scraping the lower edge of the hole into a smooth slant; it is important to keep this clean and sharp throughout any further modelling. The finished window should measure about 8 mm (⅜ in.) across and 3 mm (⅛ in.) high.

- Remove the wooden wedge with care. Press the sharp slanting edge of the sound hole (the labium) very slightly inwards, until it lies directly underneath the air canal. This edge will separate the air flow when the finished pipe is blown. Smooth the edge again if necessary.

- Make one or two finger holes in the front wall of the instrument. (A true ocarina usually has four to six holes at the front and two at the back, but it requires very delicate tuning.)

- Try the flute out. If there is no sound, try closing the air canal a little or adjusting the labium very slightly. It is important to get a clear sound while the clay is still raw. You do need to exercise a fine touch here, so children will need some help.

- Once fired, hang the pipe on a leather thong.

- Barrel flutes can also be made in the form of round-bodied animals, such as a tortoise, a bird or a fish.

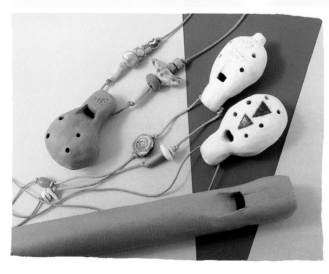

## Here's how it's done

- Using finely grogged clay, make a pinch-pot measuring approx. 8 cm (3 ⅛ in.) high and 6 cm (2 ⅜ in.) wide, with a wall thickness of about 8 mm (⅜ in.). Make the base a little wider than the top in order that it sits firmly.
- Add on bird heads or other decorative elements, according to your design.
- Using a needle or apple-corer, cut a 1.5-cm (⅝ in.) hole for the pipe through the wall of the pot, about a third of the way down.
- To make the pipe, clothe a wooden rod measur-

ing 8-10 mm (⅜ in.) in diameter with a 3 mm- (⅛ in.) thick slab of clay and smooth it off (for exact instructions, see the directions for the wind harp on p.92).
- Cut the clay off cleanly at the top edge of the pipe.
- Ease the sheath of clay gently away from the wood by squeezing lightly all over, then roll carefully on a flat surface, the rod still in place, to smooth the walls over once again.
- Cut the clay off at the bottom – once more with a clean edge – to give the pipe a length of about 8-10 cm (3¼– 4 in.).

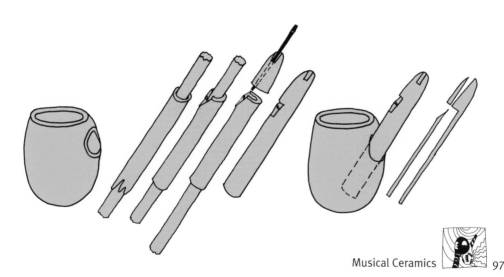

- Cut a 5 mm (¼ in.)- high window at the very top of the pipe, creating a labium with a sharp, slanting edge (see previous project).
- Make a half-sphere the size of a hazelnut for the mouthpiece, smoothly rounded at the top and cut off clean at the bottom.
- Carefully press a wooden or cardboard wedge (6 mm (¼ in.) wide, 2 mm (⅛ in.) thick at the sharpened edge) down through the centre of the mouthpiece.
- Leave both parts – mouthpiece and pipe – to dry until almost leatherhard. Push the pipe up on its supporting rod until the top just sticks clear of the wood.
- Stick the two pieces together with slip, so that the bottom of the air canal (the pointed end of the wedge) sits directly over the window in the top of the pipe and the airflow is divided by the labium.
- Gently roll the pipe once more over a wooden board and then carefully remove the rod. Pull the wedge out of the mouthpiece with equal care.
- Check the tone of the pipe. If there is no sound, try opening or closing the air canal slightly, sharpening the edge of the labium again, or manipulating the pipe shaft very gently.
- Once the pipe is leatherhard, insert it into the window in the pot, adjusting the slant of the edges if necessary. The pipe should sit fairly upright, with its lower edge just resting on the base of the pot.
- Fix the pipe into its hole with a soft coil of clay and a little slip.
- Clean and smooth all walls and joins.
- Support the pipe gently while drying to prevent any distortion.
- Glaze the body of the pot after a first biscuit firing, but ensure that the labium and mouth piece are kept clean!

*Fill the pot with a little water and blow hard or gently. The maddest sounds will come gurgling, twittering, trilling and bubbling up from inside.*

# Building with mud and clay

The various bricks and roof tiles made from fired clay, which are such a familiar sight in our latitudes, are central to our building traditions. In dryer regions of the world it is common to find constructions of unfired clay and mud, even for permanent dwellings. Perhaps the most well-known are the adobe fortresses traditional to the North American Indians, or the African mud hut. These are built either with bricks formed from mud or clay and built into walls once dry, or alternatively the soft material is built up directly over an internal frame. The clay is mixed with straw or chaff to give it lasting strength. Children take a special delight in reinterpreting such exotic dwelling types and imagining living in them, and even the very smallest nursery school children will be able to construct a simple hut.

## An African village

Following their imagination or taking inspiration from picture books, the children can construct a series of huts either by modelling the clay freely or by starting with a quick knee bowl. In addition to the clay, into which they can mix – quite authentically – strands of grass or straw, or perhaps torn strips of paper, they add can other materials to their buildings such as twigs, straw matting and rushes. The models need simply be dried in the air and then painted with ethnic motifs in coloured slip or poster paint. In no time you'll have a whole village. A brilliant activity for warm summer days!

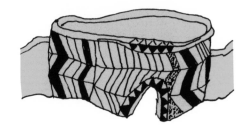

## Tip

If there happens to be a large source of natural clay loam nearby, you can experiment with building larger huts in the open air. Provide extra support for the walls with twigs and branches, and weave in lengths of fabric.

Building with Mud and Clay

## Brickworks

As with wooden building blocks, miniature bricks are only really fun to play with if you have a plentiful supply for building. An industrious task for the whole group then – or the family! Progress is relatively fast if you begin by rolling out an even slab of terracotta clay to a thickness of about 2 cm (¾ in.)and leave it to dry until almost leatherhard. Lay a ruler against a straight edge and cut strips of 2.3 cm (1 in.) in width, then cut each of these into 5 cm (2 in.)-long bricks. Try to press the knife rather than drag it: this is easier if one person holds the ruler steady while another does the cutting. The standard bricks can be varied with individually-cut columns, steps, window lintels and door arches. The truly industrious brick maker will pierce each piece eight times with a little stick. Smooth the edges with a damp sponge. The bricks need not be fired separately; instead stack them inside an earthenware pot in the kiln.

## To make mortar

Stir 50 g (2 oz) flour into 2 ml (half a teaspoon) of water. Bring to the boil and mix in 300 g (12 oz) of fine sand (e.g., the type used in bird cages). Add more water if necessary, and set about building your wall. The mortar dries quickly and will set very firmly. To dismantle a building in order to reuse the bricks, loosen the mortar by soaking in hot water.

# A haunted castle

## Here's how it's done

- Sketch out a plan for a castle, with turrets, an imposing gateway and drawbridge, windows and battlements.
- Make yourselves a supply of thick, roughly rolled coils (approx. 2–3 cm (¾ – 1 in.) across) from heavily grogged, dark clay. Lay out the ground plan with some of your coils; there is no need for a flat base.
- Build up the walls with further coils (for the basic technique, see p. 36). You can either leave openings for gateways and windows as you build, or cut them out later from the finished walls.
- Using a wooden stick or the handle of a fork, scrape vertical grooves into the coils to suggest a pattern of mortar joins and, if you like, flatten the walls a little with a wooden bat to give the appearance of sandstone blocks.
- Add on details such a window frames, turrets and battlements.
- Model some ghosts by rolling out thin slabs of white clay and draping them over the necks of bottles or similar, to dry in folds.
- If the walls of the castle are very thick in places, prick these with a needle, then leave the construction to dry.

- Before firing, pick out only a few key details, such as mortar joins, in coloured slip, in order to preserve the spooky impression of the rough-hewn walls.
- To give the effect of a true fiery glow from inside the castle, stick little sheets of transparent orange paper to the inside of the windows (e.g. lantern paper).
- Arrange tea-lights inside the castle, or even light a sparkler in the courtyard, but remember never to leave the candles burning unattended

## Some variations

A lonesome tower or a mysterious ruin both make excellent hurricane lamps for the garden. Equally simple to model either freely or from coils are fairy-tale houses; a favourite with children, who like to decorate them with endless loving detail. Why not let them try a crooked old witch's house, a round cottage from the land of the Hobbit or perhaps even a lighthouse? If the intention is to light up the house from the inside, please ensure that the children leave an open roof and enough windows and doors to create a draft for the candles. Another idea is to build play- or dolls' houses in the theme of some favourite play figures.

### Tip

Glaze any coats of arms or other applied ornament separately, in order not to have to fire the whole building a second time.

*The spooky castle gives out a really creepy glow in the darkness.*

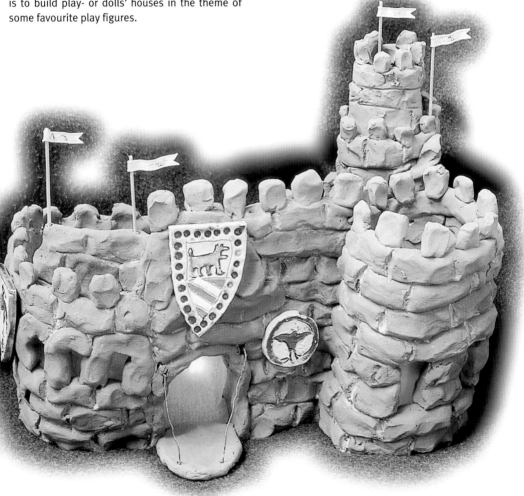

# The Glaze

## Where can we fire our pots?

For those who have no access to a kiln, some larger modelling or DIY-stores and specialist suppliers offer a firing service. Sometimes a local pottery will make their kiln available to the public, and many towns have public ceramic workshops. Whatever the solution, always make sure you have addressed the question of firing before starting on any clay project.

## What happens in the kiln?

When the thoroughly-dried wares are fired to a high temperature in the kiln, the clay undergoes a series of chemical transformations which change its basic properties. As the clay starts to glow red, the body expels a mixture of water and chemicals. When the temperature reaches 600°C the body turns rigid; the greater the heat, the more solid the body becomes. After the first firing (known as the 'biscuit' firing), at about 800°C, the body remains porous (as with terracotta, for example). With a second, higher firing, usually at around 1000°C, it becomes watertight. The only truly watertight bodies are stoneware and

*Remnants of bathroom tiles painted with an array of bright experimental glazes. Colours have been applied in dabs and splashes and painted on with brushes and slip-trailers.*

porcelain, which are fired to an even higher temperature of around 1250–1400°C.

## What is a glaze?

If we hold a biscuit-fired body under water, we immediately notice from the bubbles and fizzing, and from the colour change, that it is beginning to soak up the water: the walls are not watertight. Real tableware behaves quite differently. It is covered with a smooth, shiny coating: the glaze. Water falls straight off this surface in droplets.

The best way to understand a glaze is as a thin coating of glass. The finely-ground particles of glass are mixed to a paste with water, applied to the biscuit-fired clay body and then melted at very high temperatures in the kiln. The melting process binds the layer of glaze with the surface of the clay itself. There are many different ways of colouring the glass particles. In its raw state a glaze will often have a completely different colour to the fired result.

## Special precautions for working with children

- Never leave children to handle glazes unattended.
- Never allow any consumption of food or drink in the workshop, and ensure children put nothing in their mouths.
- Please only use lead-free glazes with a low chemical content. Manufacturers usually use the following labelling system: * = suitable for tableware; ** = for decorative use only; *** = contains lead, unsuitable for household objects.
- Store all glazes in well-labelled buckets with secure lids.
- Choose white or light-coloured glazes as a preference, in order that even a thin covering will bring good results.
- Try to ensure that the children handle the biscuit-fired bodies as little as possible, as any spots of grease or dirt will prevent the glaze from taking.

## Applying the Glaze

Stir your glaze thoroughly before use with a wooden stick until you have a thin, even solution that is free of lumps. If a glaze seems gritty, strain it through a sieve. Then follow one of the following three basic application methods, depending on the size of the object and the type of glaze:

**Method 1:**
Hold smaller pieces with the hands or with glazing tongs. With one light sweep, immerse the piece completely in the glaze and immediately lift it out.

**Method 2:**
Hold larger pieces carefully or lay them on slats of wood over a bowl, then pour the glaze over evenly with a ladle or scoop. Swish the glaze around the inside of a pot before turning it over and coating the outside.

**Method 3:**
Paint the glaze on with a soft flat brush. Only use products specifically manufactured for this purpose. Many ready-mixed glazes need to be painted on in two layers; one lengthways, then after drying another crossways over the top.

## General hints

- Touch up any air bubbles or mistakes with a brush.
- Clean any glaze from the bases of all objects with a damp sponge as soon as the surface coating has dried. If using a particularly runny glaze, wipe off an extra 5 mm (¼ in.) above the lower edge to avoid the risk of drips falling onto the kiln shelf. At the same time, use a needle to free up any openings or cut-outs which have become blocked with glaze.
- Leave glazed objects to dry for several hours before firing.
- Place round objects or anything else with an all-over glaze on special stilts (metal or ceramic) in the kiln, to prevent them from sticking.
- Take care when arranging works in the kiln that they do not touch each other or the heating elements on the side walls.

When using glazes for the first time, give the

children plenty of opportunity to practise on flat objects such as tiles and plates, where their applications will not run off so easily. Use the glaze sparingly; it is not always necessary to immerse the object completely, or to coat every inch. It can often be attractive to pick out individual details, or to combine small areas of glaze with coloured slip, thus creating pleasing contrasts between the glazed and unglazed surface. Many – although not all – glazes mix readily with others to provide a wide variety of colours across the spectrum; plenty of room for experimentation ... !

## Tip

Unsuccessful results can usually be rescued with a thin application of a darker, matt glaze. Smaller accidents on ornamental pieces can be touched up with ceramic dyes designed for baking in a domestic oven (specialist suppliers).

## Experimenting with glazes

Children love vibrant patterns: try letting them daub the glaze on with big brushes. To do this they need to stand on a chair with the work on the floor and let big splashes drop down from the brush – trying always to aim for the right spot, of course!

- Make a splatter pattern with old tooth brushes: either stroke a thumb over the bristles or drag the brush over an old kitchen grill. Drop a large dollop of thin glaze onto a surface and then tip or shake it to create a bold 'chance' pattern.
- Glaze only one half of a pot; or dip each half in a different glaze, allowing a slight overlap between the two.
- Combine sand, tiny pebbles, snippets of copper wire or little glass beads ('rocaille') with a glaze and let them melt together.
- Brush surface reliefs with several different-coloured glazes and then wipe off with a damp sponge so that only the engraved design retains the glaze.

*To create lively chance patterns on a flat surface, dab on a blob of glaze or coloured slip and immediately blow hard in all directions or tip the object back and forth.*

# Some Glazing Projects

## Molten Jewels

Please always handle glass with care. Only do this activity with older children, and do not leave them to work unattended. To break fragments of glass into smaller shards, place them in a plastic bag and smash carefully with a hammer. Remove any unused glass from the worktop straight away.

This experiment shows children just what happens when the kiln gets extremely hot. They fill flat, biscuit-fired dishes with a 5 mm (¼ in.)-high layer of kaolin powder. On top of this they arrange small shards of glass, or glass beads, in a variety of colours, placing them either singly or in little mounds. Leave a clear space around each piece or mound and dab a small amount of clear glaze in the gaps, to ensure everything moulds together well. During the glaze firing the shards melt down into an authentic-looking 'precious

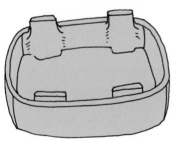

stone', either with nicely rounded or prettily fringed edges. The layer of kaolin prevents the jewel from sticking to the pottery dish, and can just be brushed off under a running tap.

### Tip

You can decorate real pebbles with dabs of coloured glaze and fire in the same way as clay.

*Inside view of the mammoth bowl from p. 28. To the side an amulet with tiny glass beads melted into the surface.*

## Secret boxes

### *Here's how it's done*

◎ Make small hollow bodies and cut them open. In the bottom half of each place four little supports against the inside edge for the lid to rest on later. Decorate the outside of the lid with engraved designs or with personal 'coats of arms'. Inscribe the walls of the body inside and out with a secret code, phrases in a foreign language, or private messages. Leave both halves to dry on top of each other, placing a little kitchen paper between the rims to stop them from sticking together.

◎ After a first firing, glaze the inside of each half with bold colours and designs. For example, dab on different glazes and stir them into a marble pattern with a little stick. Or melt blue or multi-coloured shards of glass into a reflective lake (ask at a glaziers, or use fragments of coloured bottles or sea glass). Fired to a normal glazing temperature, the shards will form a surface of blistered craters; at a stoneware temperature they will melt into a smooth, transparent layer of colour, crazed with tiny cracks.

*The little boxes are decorated beautifully inside and out. Above left, a dish filled with kaolin powder in which the 'jewels' have been melted.*

## Hang up your coat to the sound of the sea

These stunning sea scenes are best painted on unglazed, biscuit-fired tiles available from any tile shop, or on slabs of your own making. Equally suitable are remnants of bathroom tiles in a matt white glaze. Incidentally, the latter make economical surfaces for experimenting with various glaze techniques.

### Here's how it's done

- Lay out several unglazed tiles.
- In a large yoghurt pot mix up about 3 dessert-spoons of a bright blue or turquoise glaze with half a teaspoon of washing-up liquid.
- Blow firmly into the mixture through a straw until a thick foam begins to form. Please don't suck on the straw and swallow any of the solution!
- As the foam begins to rise over the top of the yoghurt pot, spread it quickly onto the tile with the spoon. The bubbles will immediately start to burst and form delicate patterns. Be careful not take too much foam, or you will be just left with a series of dark blotches.

- Allow the bubble patterns to dry.
- Paint on sea animals in bold glazes (yellow, red, orange, brown) with a thin brush or a slip trailer. It is best to stick to simple, recognisable forms such as a whale, an octopus, star fish or sea horses.
- Once the glazed tiles have been fired, you can group them together on a plain or brightly-lacquered wooden board, adding further pieces of driftwood for decoration if you wish. Screw the board to a wall and add hooks for the children's coats.

### Tips

- Soap-bubble patterns also work very well with coloured slip; glaze and slip can be combined in a single process and firing.

## Designing with stencils

Cut out (or tear) simple designs with clear outlines from stiff paper or thick plastic film. Lay the stencils on unglazed tiles and hold firmly or stick in place with double-sided tape. Using a sponge or paintbrush, carefully dab glaze or coloured slip over the design. Remove the stencil and allow the decoration to dry. For really lively scenes, apply several layers of stencils in different colours. You can also glaze the edges of the tiles. Put the tiles through a glaze firing and turn them into attractive table mats by sticking four wooden beads or little slabs of cork to their bases.

## More design solutions

### Under-glaze colours

These pigments come in individual blocks in boxes like poster paints. They are mixed up with water or a painting medium and applied with a paintbrush, but are only suitable for older children. Paint onto biscuit-fired bodies, fire and coat with a transparent glaze.

## Applying colour after firing

- Not all biscuit-fired works need necessarily be glazed, providing they are not intended as tableware. Here are a few alternative finishes:
- Nursery-school children will love to paint decorative objects with simple poster paints or watercolours. For a more durable finish, use acrylics.
- If you rub a smooth clay surface with a little hand cream, floor wax, or coloured shoe polish, it will become darker and take on a soft sheen and will mark less easily. Please only use environmentally-friendly products that are safe for children. Apply the paste with a brush and polish up with a soft cloth.
- For a pre-historic look you can decorate white or cream-coloured surfaces with natural plant

dies. Beetroot juice, boiled-up green walnut casings, or spinach, curry powder, onion skins etc. boiled in a little water; all these are worth trying. Traditional dye-woods (red, blue and yellow in colour) produce a bolder effect, as do manufactured plant dyes such as kermes berries (a type of oak), blueberry juice and others. Bear in mind however that none of these are particularly durable or light-resistant. Polish up afterwards with bees wax.

# It Comes Around Every Year: ceramic creations for seasonal events and festivities

## Christmas and Festivals of Lights

### Candle-holders

Hollow out a ball of clay and press the top edge into a wide flat lip. Carve this into a star shape or other decorative motif. Leave the pot to dry upside down and when ready place a perfumed tea-light in the middle. Another idea is to model an oil-lamp like the ones described on p.40 and decorate it with a nice fat star around the wick-holder.

### Hanging decorations

Make a mobile of stars cut from a marbled mixture of different-coloured clay scraps. Hang these from delicate threads on a knotty branch. Alternatively, cut a variety of motifs from a slab of clay with biscuit cutters and hang them from a cord stretched across a window.

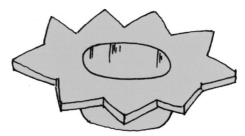

### Incense tree

Cut a quarter-circle with a radius of approx. 25 cm (10 in.) from a 1cm (⅜ in.)-thick slab of clay. Join the edges into a cone shape and leave to dry on another cone of newspaper. When leatherhard, cut holes in the walls with an apple-corer. Model decorations from soft clay in some favourite shapes: hearts, gingerbread men, stars, bells etc. Stick these to the

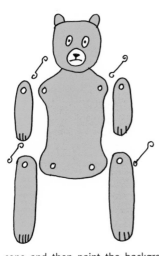

cone and then paint the background with green-coloured slip. Place a large cut-out star on top of the tree. Fire once and then glaze the decorations colourfully and fire again. Place a glowing incense cone in a saucer or a tea-light holder and set it under the tree. This idea works well for other seasonal motifs such as snowmen, angels, Father Christmas, etc.

## Tooth-breaking gingerbread

Roll out a slab of terracotta clay to a thickness of about 1cm (⅜ in.) and cut out traditional gingerbread men and other motifs. Use a slip trailer to 'ice' the shapes prettily with white slip. Make hanging holes and thread onto colourful ribbon to decorate the Christmas tree or festive branches.

## Other ideas

- Using the techniques for modelling cone figures on p.89, make a miniature nativity scene with sheep and cows and arrange it in a clay dish.
- Make cane tops (see p.54) in the shape of stars, faces or other festive motifs. Fix them to canes adorned with coloured ribbon and tinsel.
- Model a dish for sweets and biscuits by first cutting out a circular slab of clay and then giving it a frilly edge. Drape it over an upturned soup plate to dry, and decorate as you wish.

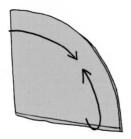

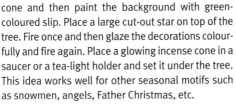

## Easter

### Filled eggs

Model two matching oval-shaped thumb bowls which will fit together once dry. Fill with a miniature clay figure such as a chick or Easter bunny. Don't fire; just decorate colourfully with poster paints. As an alternative, you can model bigger versions of these oval bowls and glaze the insides with bright Easter motifs.

### Treasure horn

Model a horn like the one intended for earwigs (p.84) and glaze it with bright spring-inspired patterns. Fill with goodies and hide it in a tree to be found by little hunters.

### Birds' nests

Weave thin coils of clay loosely into a basket shape. Once dry, fill with moss, lichen or straw and a collection of Easter eggs.

### Easter bunnies

Model terracotta cane-tops in the shape of rabbits and set them leaping through the grass: sow wheatgrass in a simple flower pot and give it 8-10 days to reach a good height before adding your bunnies.

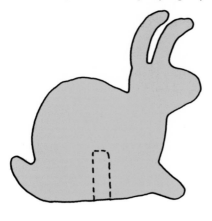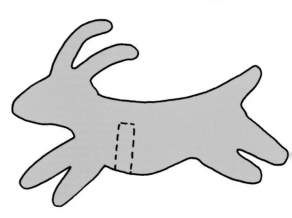

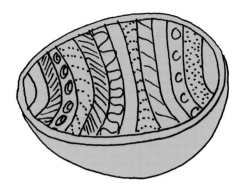

## Gifts, school fairs and other occasions

- Clay instruments such as maracas, wind harps and prettily decorated bells are always well received.
- Tea bowls with accompanying mottos or recipe cards for different herbal teas.
- Herb bunches adorned with bird- or star-topped sticks.
- All-purpose dishes speedily modelled from slabs. These are most effective if you make them generously sized and brightly glazed.
- Attractive soap-dishes.
- Jewellery in all manner of designs.

*An array of attractive little trinkets made from simple clay balls.*

## Activities for birthday parties, school festivities or ceramic days

- Each child makes their own self-portrait bust.
- The group works together to produce a ceramic frieze depicting a particular theme.
- Everyone will enjoy the 'paradise island' activity described on p.13.
- Little competitions with individual prizes: who can make the most beautiful hen, the wackiest tea-bowl or the highest tower?
- Disguised objects: each member of the group covers a sturdy object such as an old toy, a telephone book or a garden trowel, in a layer of clay. Others then have to guess the object from the look and feel of the just-visible outline.
- Lucky dip: bury the prizes in a large lump of clay so that each participant has to dig in and excavate with their hands.
- Set up a stall selling your own ceramic wares.
- Everyone joins in with games such as seeing how far they can throw a lump of clay, bowling with clay skittles, or the touch-memory game (p.59).
- Make-up session: Instead of face-paints, the children paint each other with clay slip, transforming themselves into American Indians or living sculptures.
- An exhibition of works in a romantic setting, such as the school courtyard, or amongst plants in the garden.
- A group firing session with a simple home-made kiln. To keep up interest you may want to bake pizzas or bread in the oven while it is heating up.

# Firing

## Building simple kilns

Nothing in the whole pottery process is quite as exciting as the direct experience of a firing: fire, smoke, action, waiting; seeing and touching the transformation process as it occurs. You will need to set aside at least one whole day for the event. The improvised kilns that we describe on these pages will bring quite unpredictable results and are in no way suitable for glaze firings, but despite their simplicity are perfectly adequate for biscuit firings. On removal from the kiln, the clay bodies will definitely have changed colour, will ring clear and will no longer dissolve if immersed in water.

Detailed instructions can be found in specialist literature or on the Internet for anyone wanting to build the well-known saw-dust kilns, to set up an open firing in a ditch or even to construct a more intricate, permanent kiln from bricks or fire-proof stone. In the field of experimental archaeology too, there is a wealth of academic research into the history of kilns before the advent of electricity. Please bear in mind when carrying out any of our instructions that building a kiln can never be as exact a process as following a simple cookery recipe. So much depends upon the available construction materials and how they behave in the heat, local environmental conditions and the weather, the type of clay you are using, etc. All these and other

related factors mean that you will always need to be prepared to improvise and to exercise a certain experimental instinct. In addition you need always to be prepared for accidents and unsuccessful firings where the works may simply explode or fail to solidify, and it is best to warn the children of this possibility in advance. For this reason it is important to plan enough other attractions alongside the firing so that the day remains a success. For instance, you could decorate the outside of the kiln with coloured slip, or bake flat loaves next to the hot chimney.

## What to fire

Choose a coarse, well blended clay which will not shrink so badly in the heat and can withstand temperature variations much better than a finer body. Let the children start by modelling two or three small, compact pieces no larger than fist size, such as little bowls, sphere shapes and rounded animals modelled from one piece. Ensure that the walls are of an even thickness and tap firmly with a spoon or a wooden bat to compress them further. This gives them a smoother density and results in fewer breakages. Polish the objects or decorate with engraved patterns, but avoid any fiddly applica-

tions. All the works must be thoroughly dried out before they go in the kiln. Even better is to heat them up slowly in a kitchen oven or on the outer surface of the kiln so that they reach a temperature of 100-200°C before going in the kiln. Always use metal tongs or oven gloves to transport the work; never touch them with your bare hands!

## Preparations and safety measures

The home-made kiln requires a large area in the open air where the participants can operate freely without getting in each other's way and at a safe distance from the fire. Consider also the effects of smoke on neighbours and neighbouring nature (e.g. birds' nests), and ensure you comply with the legal restrictions relating to open fires. Always build the kiln outside, never in an enclosed space. Keep any flammable materials well away from the scene and be careful not to build too close to trees, bushes or dry meadows. Please restrict yourselves to smaller models which do not waste materials in order that the project is as ecologically sustainable as possible.

The ground beneath the kiln should be protected with a sheet of iron (an old baking tray will do) or a layer of bricks. The models we suggest function best on a warm, dry and preferably still day. Make sure the children are well briefed before the process and all movements are well understood. They must have all the safety precautions explained to them and be suitably dressed for the day, wearing natural fibres and sturdy shoes, with long hair tied back, and gloves where appropriate. Each child is allotted a specific task in advance of the firing, so that everyone is occupied and knows what the others are doing: some can collect and look after the firewood; others will observe and stoke the fire, or mark out a safety line and ensure people stay outside of the zone; you will also need people in charge of water buckets, etc. In this way even the youngest will feel fully involved, even if they can't take part in the actual firing process. Always keep buckets of water and sand handy, and if possible also a protective metal sheet in case of gusts of wind (flying sparks!).

*A kiln constructed from old bricks. The fire is kept alight for several hours.*

The best time to hold the firing is in the afternoon and into the evening, so that the spectacular optical effects of the fire and glowing interior can be appreciated to the full. Most kilns (with the exception of the newspaper one) need to be left for several hours to cool off before the wares can be removed. Please never leave any kiln unattended!

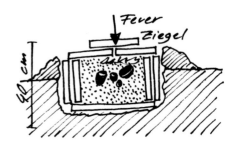

## The firing process

Two fundamental principles define the type of firing that takes place in a kiln: either it is a process of oxidisation, or of reduction. The former involves a constant flow of oxygen drawn in by an open flame and requires a continuous supply of wood or other material for the fire. The reduction process on the other hand works by shutting off the air supply and depriving the fire of oxygen, allowing the embers to burn away slowly with a gentle glow but without developing an open flame. The bodies resulting from this type of firing are often blackened in appearance or with a smoky pattern.

The chief difficulty in constructing one's own kiln is to create sufficient heat; a normal bonfire or even a pizza oven will not reach a high enough temperature for firing clay. It is possible to gauge the temperature roughly from the colour of the glowing fire. For example, a dark red indicates that the fire has reached approx. 700°C; pale red 800; pale orange 1000, and a white flame approx. 1200°C. However, these last two stages will certainly not be attained in any of our home-made designs.

## The sawdust kiln

- Dig a square pit in the ground measuring about 20 cm (8 in.) deep and 50 x 50 cm (19 x 19 in.) across.
- Lay two flat terracotta roof tiles in the bottom of the pit. (Normal, fire-proof bricks can also be used for the whole construction instead of roof tiles.)
- Prop up a further two tiles lengthways along the edge of each wall of the pit, so that you end up with a sort of double-walled box.
- Build a little earth up around the walls for insulation, but leave the gaps in the side open a little, in order to allow a small amount of ventilation around the structure.
- Pack the chamber tightly with fine and middle-

grade sawdust from untreated wood (no recycled wood, chipboard or other!). Pack the wares to be fired with further sawdust and lay them in the upper third of the filled chamber.
- Top the sawdust with a layer of screwed-up newspaper, straw or other easily flammable material.
- Light the paper in several places and cover it with a lid of two further roof tiles as soon as the sawdust has begun to smoulder.
- Check after a couple of minutes that the sawdust has begun to glow and light again if necessary. There will not yet be any real flame; the only way to detect the internal process will be from the fine coils of smoke and from the conducted heat.
- Leave the kiln to get on with its job for several hours. Sometimes it can take a whole day for all the sawdust to smoulder away. Remove the lid only when there is no more smoke and the kiln has cooled to a luke-warm temperature. Your fired wares will come out of the kiln with a lasting blackened appearance.

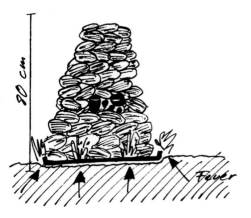

## The beehive

- You will need a large pile of old newspapers, weighing several kilos (4–5 lb). Open out the newspapers and smooth the pages flat.
- Lay four pages on top of each other and twist lengthways into a tight strand. Attach further sheets and carry on twisting in the same way until you have a paper strand approx. 5 cm (2 in.) thick and 1m (39 in.) long.
- Prepare three of these strands to start with, and set the children to work making more for later.
- Twist your first three strands together at one end and work them into a thick plait. Attach further strands when you come to the end of these and continue with your plait until it measures 3 m (10 feet).
- Laying the plait on its side, coil it into a tight, flat spiral. Lay this on a heat-resistant base such as a baking tray or other metal sheet.
- Make a second spiral according to the same method and lay this on top of the first.
- Make three to four plaited spirals, each one a little smaller than the last, and layer them up to create a dome shape.
- Lay the works to be fired (pre-heated in the kitchen oven if possible) in the centre and on top of the double base layer.
- Fill any gaps in the construction if necessary with further balls of screwed up newspaper until the walls are compact and sturdy.

*Above: plaiting the paper twists. Below: the massive beehive kiln open and ready to receive the clay bodies.*

*Two varieties of kiln: the 'beehive' on the left is set alight in several places, while the paper and clay kiln on the right is fired with wood and burns for many hours. While the newspaper on the exterior turns to ash, a red-hot glow continues to burn inside.*

- Replace the dome back on the base layer of spirals.
- If the construction still seems a little unstable, secure it with some thin wire.
- Light the paper walls in several places around the base. (Please only operate this kiln on truly still days or the resulting ash will be blown far and wide.) After the first real flames the dome will burn gently for another couple of hours with an even glow and little smoke until reduced to a small pile of ashes. It only remains to reclaim your fired wares from the ashes, and you will see that the glowing paper alone has actually produced enough heat for a successful firing.

## A simple paper and clay kiln

- Dig a hollow in the ground measuring about 70 x 30 cm (28 x 12 in.) and with a depth of 20 cm (8 in.). The longer sides should lie parallel to the direction of the prevailing wind.
- Make a base with a baking sheet or a layer of bricks.
- In the back half of the pit (that will later be out of the wind) insert a metal grill, whether an old oven grill, a bicycle basket or even a piece of

chicken wire. This is where you will place your pottery pieces for firing. Preferably place a further baking sheet under this or a layer of loam, in order that the grill does not stand directly in the fire.
- Around this metal grill build up a tipi-like scaffold out of 1m (3 feet)-long branches and twigs, old wooden battens or other untreated long scraps of wood. Ram the ends down well into the earth so that they will hold steady, and stabilise with a ring of wire at the top and bottom.
- Mix up about 20 kg (45 lb) of clay or loam with an additional 30% sand, sawdust or other fine particles and stir in tubs to a thick slurry.
- The walls of the tipi are constructed from sheets of firm paper (brown paper, old magazines etc.) pasted with the clay slurry. Take sheets of roughly A3 size and paint the paste on thinly with a sponge or with the hands. Drape the sheets, clay sides innermost, around the stick frame, building the layers out like a curtain over the open half of the hollow (this will be the future fire pit). Strengthen the lower edge further by shovelling some earth a little way up the sides.
- In order to create a firm structure for our models, we used cotton cloths painted on both sides with

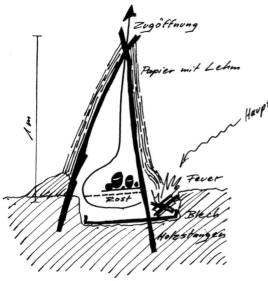

Zugöffnung

Papier mit Lehm

Hauptwindrichtung

1 m

Feuer

Rost

Blech

Holzstangen

- Leave an opening of about 5 cm (2 in.) at the top of the frame to create a draught for the fire.
- Fill the fire pit with newspaper, sawdust or small dry twigs and then set alight. The kiln can be set in operation while the walls are still damp.

  Keep replenishing the fire with a supply of dry sticks and wood over the following three to four hours. You will not need huge amounts; more important is a good draught and an even glow, and you never want the flames to reach as high as the opening at the top. On a really still day the children may need to fan the fire a little to create a good draught. The aim is to create sufficient heat so that the walls actually bake hard on the inside and a colour change can be perceived from the outside.
- Should the walls tear at any point they can be patched with a further application of clay and paper.
- Allow the oven to cool completely before removing the fired works. Please bear in mind that as the works in this model are closer to the flame they are more liable to crack than in the previous designs.

the clay slurry for the very first layer, in place of paper. This prevented the walls from tearing and meant that the children did not have to take too much care when building up the further layers.

- Apply about 10 layers in total and smooth them down firmly, allowing all members of the group to join in together.

*These are the fired works from three types of kiln – notice how some have a blackened appearance. The most spectacular was the amazing beehive oven.*

# A glance over the rim of the plate: playful designs with clay and loam

## Stone Age art on stones

The famous cave paintings which we are all familiar with from pictures originated many thousands of years ago. The prehistoric artists made many of their decorative paints from different types of ground-up earth which they then formed into chalks or mixed with various sticky materials such as egg white, beer or milk, and applied either with the fingers or with a blow pipe. Search out flat stones and other found objects on which to create your own prehistoric designs.

To make your own paints, dry out some balls of clay in different colours, then crush to a fine powder inside plastic bags. Mix these powders to a paste with a little milk, and paint on to the stones with fingers or brushes made from tufts of grass, or try blowing through straws. Animal portraits, hunting scenes, stick people or abstract scenes will all give an authentic prehistoric look.

## Body painting and living statues

These activities will only work outdoors where any mess can be cleaned up and on a hot summer's day! Wash-tubs full of water or a garden hose are essential. For a war-painting session in the style of the American Indians, first mix up a thick paste from fine unblended clay mixed with some cooking oil and water. Apply a thick cream or body lotion all over the skin, and then paint the clay paste on with the fingers. Alternatively, the children can smear soft clay all over each other and experiment with altering their body shapes (avoiding eyes, mouth, nose and ears). Or several mud-people can arrange themselves into a living sculpture, ensuring someone remains clean enough to document the project with photographs!

## Decorative clay paper

Old-fashioned sugar paper can be painted with a soft clay paste or coloured clay powders just as effectively as with watercolours, resulting in some superb naturalistic effects. There is endless scope here for the children's creative imagination and the resulting decorative papers are versatile and durable.

The clay pastes and paints are made by mixing soft clay into a solution of wall-paper paste (made up according to the manufacturer's instructions) or a home-made flour and water glue.

Flour and water glue: Stir 100 g (4 oz) flour into approx. 0.3l (1 fl. oz) cold water until any lumps have disappeared. Bring a litre of water to the boil in a saucepan, mix in the flour paste and allow it to simmer for five minutes, stirring constantly. Leave the mixture to cool, stirring intermittently. Add a few spoonfuls of very soft or powdered clay and stir briskly until you have a thick paste with a uniform consistency.

comb or a cardboard scraper, or simply the fingers, drag a design through the layer of clay paste. With grogged (blended) clay the surface will dry to a rough, earthy appearance, and with ungrogged the effect will be finer, but still three-dimensional. Draw the papers over the edge of a table to flatten them out if necessary and either hang on the wall or use to decorate boxes, scrapbooks and folders.

## The Zen garden

A paste mixed up with dark, heavily grogged clay and applied to white card results in some very authentic looking Japanese-garden effects. First paint on the paste as for the above decorative papers but leaving a thicker layer. Then, just as the real Zen gardens of Japan are raked into regular lines and graceful curves, so you proceed to trail similar patterns through the paste with a comb or cardboard scraper. For an additional effect you can also stick small flat pebbles into the wet paste, which in the art of the Far East represent islands in a sea of waves.

Apply the clay paste in a 1mm (¹⁄₁₆ in.)- thick layer onto sturdy sugar paper, using fat brushes and mixing shades as you wish. If the paste does not cover the paper thickly enough, add a little more clay to the mixture. You will achieve an even more colourful effect if you wash or splatter the paper with inks or watercolours before painting with clay. Using a thick

# Glossary of specialist terms

**Biscuit-firing**: The first firing of the raw, thoroughly dried-out wares, reaching around 800°C. The biscuit-fired wares remain porous and ready for the application of a glaze.

**Body**: The term used for any type of clay in its raw, plastic form.

**Bone hard**: when the raw body is fully dried-out and no longer malleable. Most clay bodies will be noticeably paler at this stage than in their plastic state.

**Bronzite**: a specialist glaze, producing a bronze-coloured surface with a metallic shimmer.

**Embellishment**: the process of sticking decorative and additional elements to the basic form – e.g., handles, facial features, etc.

**Engobe (coloured slip)**: a runny slip with added dyes which is applied to the raw wares before the first firing. The colours intensify during firing.

**Glaze firing**: the second firing of the ceramic wares after an application of glaze on the biscuit-fired body. Depending on the type of clay and the glaze in question, the temperature is raised to between 1000°C and 1400°C.

**Greasy clay**: fine, ungrogged clay which is greasy to the touch. These fine masses are more suited for modelling on a wheel. They shrink more readily than the coarser, grogged types.

**Grog**: tiny milled particles of fired clay mixed into greasy masses to increase stability and malleability.

**Hand building**: the process of modelling by hand, as opposed to turning pots on a wheel or pouring into a plaster mould.

**Kanthal wire**: a specialist heatproof wire which will not contort in the kiln. Can be inserted into the raw clay, for example to attach small decorative elements.

**Kaolin**: white porcelain clay; also available in powder form.

**Kidney**: a kidney-shaped metal or wood scraper used for smoothing the walls of pots.

**Leatherhard**: once the modelled clay has been left to dry for several hours (or several days in the case of larger pieces), it has lost its plasticity but remains cool and damp to the touch and with no significant change in colour. This is the perfect stage for any engraving or polishing. Leatherhard pieces can still be joined effectively with slip, without any danger of them separating later.

**Open-air firing**: a simple firing carried out without a kiln in a pit dug in the earth or on a large bonfire.

**Open clay**: the coarse, grogged type of clay masses which are slightly dry to the touch and perfectly suited to modelling by hand. Even larger objects remain sturdy and shrink less when made from this type of clay.

**Oxide or oxide powder**: a superfine metallic powder, mixed with water and applied to relief patterns to bring out their three-dimensional form. The most common varieties are Copper Oxide (for greenish tints) and Iron Oxide (red).

**Oxidisation**: the most common firing process taking, place in an electric kiln and involving a plentiful supply of oxygen. (The opposite of reduction-firing.)

**Paper clay**: clay strengthened with paper fibres, enabling the modelling of intricate, filigree sculptures. Prepared in the studio or available ready-made at specialist suppliers.

**Plasticity**: the extent to which the clay is malleable and lends itself to shaping and modelling.

**Porous**: the vessel walls will still soak up water.

**Raw firing**: another term for the first, or biscuit, firing.

**Ready-mixed glazes: glaze solutions** prepared to a standard consistency. Most of these products are easily applied with a paintbrush.

**Reduction-firing**: the process whereby the supply of oxygen to the kiln is cut off during firing, resulting in ceramic bodies with a blackened appearance. Glazes develop differently in a reduction firing to the way they do under oxidisation.

**Resting**: leaving the clay for a short while after the initial modelling so that it is no longer quite so soft and wet, but still malleable. In the case of small pieces, the resting period need only be 15 minutes or so, while larger pieces will need longer depending on their size.

**Shards**: broken fragments of clay.

**Shrinkage**: the extent to which the clay will shrink during drying and firing. In the process any mass will lose between 10% and 20% of its original volume.

**Sintering**: the chemical transformation that takes place in a clay body in the heat of the kiln. The walls turn partially to glass and thus become watertight.

**Slip**: a soft, sloppy clay solution used for sticking on additional elements to the main piece. It is best to prepare a batch of slip in advance and keep it handy in screw-top jars. Take a small amount of clay scraps and mix to a smooth paste with water.

**Slip trailer**: a small rubber vessel with a thin spout for applying the runny coloured slip in fine lines or spots.

**Stoneware**: special types of clay mass and glazes which are fired to a higher temperature (around 1250°C) and result in a particularly hard, durable ceramic body.

**Terracotta**: the general term used for unglazed, porous-walled objects made from red-coloured clays.

**Trivet**: small metal stand for supporting objects with an all-over glaze during firing. It prevents the melting glaze from sticking to the kiln interior.

**Under-glaze colours**: Fine pigments for painting delicate patterns on white surfaces.

# Bibliography

Atkin, Jacqui *Pottery Basics*. London: A&C Black.

Bliss, Gill *Potter's Question and Answer Book*. London: A&C Black

Clough, Peter *Clay in the Primary School*. London: A&C Black.

Clough, Peter *Sculptural Materials in the Classroom*. London: A&C Black.

French, Neal *Potter's Directory of Shape and Form*. London: A&C Black

Hardy, Michael *Coiling*. London: A&C Black.

Hardy, Michael *Handbuilding*. London: A&C Black.

Magson, Mal and Chris Utley, *Exploring Clay with Children*. London: A&C Black.

White, Mary *Lettering on Ceramics*. London: A&C Black.

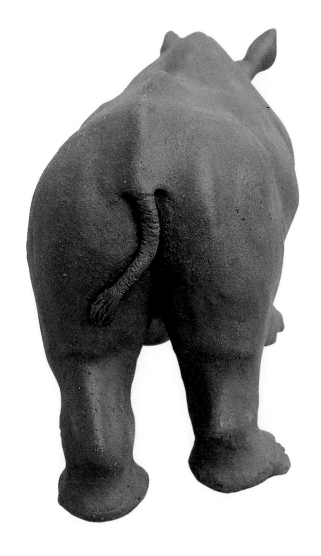

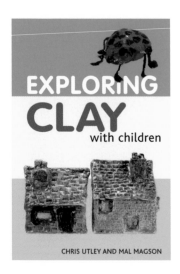
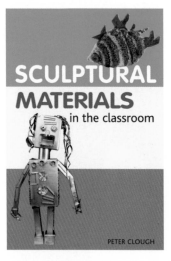